A NEW WAY OF MAKING FOWRE PARTS IN COUNTERPOINT BY THOMAS CAMPION

AND

RULES HOW TO COMPOSE BY GIOVANNI COPRARIO

Music Theory in Britain, 1500–1700: Critical Editions

A New Way of Making Fowre Parts in Counterpoint

By Thomas Campion

and

Rules how to Compose

By Giovanni Coprario

Edited and with an Introduction by
CHRISTOPHER R. WILSON

ASHGATE

Published by

Ashgate Publishing Limited
Gower House
Croft Road
Aldershot
Hants GU11 3HR
England

Ashgate Publishing Company
Suite 420
101 Cherry Street
Burlington, VT 05401-4405
USA

Ashgate website: http://www.ashgate.com

British Library Cataloguing in Publication Data
Campion, Thomas, 1567–1620
 A new way of making fowre parts in counterpoint. Rules how
 to compose. – (Music theory in Britain, 1500–1700. Critical
 editions)
 1. Music theory – Early works to 1800 2. Counterpoint – Early
 works to 1800 3. Vocal music – Early works to 1800
 4. Composition (Music) – Early works to 1800
 I. Title II. Coperario, John, 1570 (ca.) –1626. Rules how to
 compose III. Wilson, Christopher
 781.1'09032

Library of Congress Cataloging-in-Publication Data
Campion, Thomas, 1567–1620.
 A new way of making fowre parts in counterpoint by Thomas Campion and rules how to
 compose by Giovanni Coprario ; edited by Christopher R. Wilson.
  p. cm. -- (Music theory in Britain, 1500-1700)
 Includes bibliographical references and index.
 ISBN 0-7546-0515-9 (alk. paper)
  1. Counterpoint. 2. Music theory--England--History--17th century. I. Wilson,
Christopher R., 1952- II. Title. III. Series.

MT55.C17 2002
781.2'86--dc21

2002018518

ISBN 0 7546 0515 9

Typeset in Times New Roman by Bookcraft Ltd, Stroud, Gloucestershire and printed in Great Britain by MPG Books Ltd., Bodmin, Cornwall.

Contents

List of Figures

All figures by permission of the British Library, 1042.d.36(2)

Series Editor's Preface

The purpose of this series is to provide critical editions of music theory in Britain (primarily England, but Scotland, Ireland, and Wales also) from 1500 to 1700. By 'theory' is meant all sorts of writing about music, from textbooks aimed at the beginner to treatises written for a more sophisticated audience. These foundational texts have immense value in revealing attitudes, ways of thinking, and even vocabulary crucial for understanding and analyzing music. They reveal beliefs about the power of music, its function in society, and its role in education, and they furnish valuable information about performance practice and about the context of performance. They are a window into musical culture every bit as important as the music itself.

The editions in this series present the text in its original form. That is, they retain original spelling, capitalization and punctuation, as well as certain salient features of the type, for example, the choice of font. A textual commentary in each volume offers an explication of difficult or unfamiliar terminology as well as suggested corrections of printing errors; the introduction situates the work and its author in a larger historical context.

Jessie Ann Owens
Dean of Arts and Sciences
Louis, Frances and Jeffrey Sachar Professor of Music
Brandeis University

Preface

Campion's relatively short music treatise is one of a series of English treatises that appeared between 1560 and 1630 (see Introduction). All these contain ideas and theory that are to be found replicated in one or more treatises, but some yield unique points. Campion's is no exception, although its special features appear more radical than those of other treatises. It is closely linked with Coprario's *Rules how to Compose*, which was probably written before Campion's work.

These English music treatises are of great interest and potential value to scholars specialising in early modern music theory. It is surprising, therefore, that Campion's is not more readily available. It has been published in the two collected works editions alongside his poems, masques and other works, but not in its original form, nor with the benefit of Simpson's annotations, nor with the Coprario close at hand for reference. It is not available in a separate edition.

Interest in Campion's works in general and this music treatise in particular was revived in the early twentieth century. The treatise first saw the light of day in Percival Vivian's edition of the complete works of Campion (Oxford: Clarendon Press, 1909; repr. 1966, 1967). Vivian's presentation is virtually a facsimile version, retaining the original spelling and obsolete music notation, but also preserving the errors and idiosyncrasies of the original, such as the division of several music examples in score over page turns. He inadvertently introduces a number of errors and changes of his own. His commentary is very brief ('Notes', pp. 370–71) and there is little or no reference to the treatise in his Introduction.

Walter R. Davis included the treatise in his edition of the songs, masques, treatises and selection of the Latin verse (New York: Doubleday & Co., 1967; London: Faber, 1969), pp. 319–56. He modernised spelling, edited punctuation and updated the music notation but provided a less than accurate text (especially of the music examples; his errors are indicated in the footnotes). Moreover, his commentary (pp. 320–23), like Vivian's, is extremely short. In the 1970 Norton paperback edition, Davis replaced his inaccurate text with a quasi-facsimile edition.

The major points raised by Campion are discussed in the Introduction, as is the vexed question of the precise date of the treatise and its relationship to Coprario's *Rules how to Compose*. Endnotes to the text add to that discussion and point the reader to specific references.

In addition to its historical importance, the treatise offers insights into Campion the man and musician. Just as in his treatise on prosodic theory, his *Observations* (1602), Campion introduces radical thinking into Renaissance conventionality. He is a self-conscious writer working in a time of change when

Renaissance theory in both poetry and music was being challenged. He rises to that challenge and attempts to demonstrate his approach in both theory and practice. In poetic theory, the traditional pragmatists, notably Samuel Daniel and Thomas Nashe, immediately questioned, nay dismissed, Campion's standpoint, and the quest for 'measured verse' petered out. In music theory, no such response was forthcoming and in fact Campion's treatise found favour, certainly in England, over the succeeding forty years.

It is clear from the treatise that Campion was reasonably well read in music theory and aware of contemporary trends. He is dismissive of what he regards as overly complex theory (notably hexachords), and supportive of simple, clear practice. He dislikes 'intricate' polyphony, 'bated with fuge' in many parts, and advocates transparent harmony for four or fewer voices in a mainly homorhythmic style. In his own compositions he does not advance as far as Ferrabosco or Lanier in their declamatory ayres, nor does he introduce the Italian *recitativo*, but his ayres are remarkably fluid in their restrained counterpoint.

The treatise articulates as it were several aspects of Campion's compositional style. It helps explain his preference for the solo lute ayre and the simple polyphony of the part-song arrangements of the ayres from *Two Bookes*. As far as we know, Campion was not a professional lutenist, but the references to the lute in his preface on the scale indicate that he possessed a basic knowledge of the instrument as both theorist and performer. (He also refers, but only in passing, to the viol da gamba.) The inclusion of several examples from his second, third and fourth books of ayres provides a direct link between the treatise and the books of ayres. Moreover, the polyphonic 'church' music in the treatise recalls Campion's interest in divine and moral songs as presented in the first book of ayres, published in both solo and part-song versions.

Bukofzer's opinion that Campion stumbled across his radical theory about the fundamental bass by chance rather than through progressive logic because he was an amateur musician is severe. Campion may not have held a post at court or earned his living by teaching music, but his best compositions rank among the more accomplished lute songs of the period, and his comparatively large and diverse output is consistently good. Campion arrived at his theory by digesting what had been written, simplifying the progression of voices and recognising the vertical nature of parts, identifying the bass as the lowest and true foundation of the rest. Again, this approach derives from practice since in a lute song the 'tenor', if it could be discerned, does not have the same structural significance as in Renaissance vocal polyphony, especially, for example, in cantus-firmus technique. Instead, the (treble) melody and bass dictate the music of the song and thereby the harmony and various cadences, as Campion makes clear in his treatise.

In preparing this edition of Campion's treatise, together with Coprario's, I am particularly grateful to Professor John Caldwell (Music Faculty, Oxford

University) for his astute reading of the typescript and for many valuable suggestions for its improvement. I am also hugely indebted to Mr John Wagstaff (Library, Music Faculty, Oxford University) for his meticulous scrutiny of the early draft of the edition.

I should like to thank Mr Gordon Munro (Glasgow University) for information freely proffered on early Scottish psalters and the psalm tune 'Old Common'; and Professor Janet Pollack (University of Puget Sound) for her advice on schematic tonality in early seventeenth-century English keyboard sources.

The late Howard Ferguson (Cambridge) kindly read a draft of the typescript and made important comments, especially concerning early seventeenth-century English musical practice.

In August 2000 I was awarded a British Academy Research Grant and was very pleased to be able to appoint Mr Alexander Binns (St Anne's College, Oxford) as a research assistant. His contribution to the final stages of the project has been extensive and invaluable. I should also like to acknowledge receipt of a small grant from the Research Endowment Trust Fund of the University of Reading which enabled me to get the project under way in the first place in 1997.

I am grateful to the British Library for permission to reproduce the illustrations, and to the Huntington Library, San Marino, CA, for permission to edit the Coprario treatise. Thanks also to my commissioning editor, Rachel Lynch, for her support and encouragement throughout.

Any errors which occur in the final version of the text are, of course, entirely my responsibility.

Christopher R. Wilson

Introduction

Background to Campion

Thomas Campion (1567–1620) was an English Renaissance neoclassical Latin poet, an English lyric poet, a composer of lute ayres, a literary and musical theorist, and the author of several courtly masques.[1] A significant number of twentieth-century scholars have preferred to concentrate on Campion's English poetry and lute songs, in particular the five books of ayres for which he composed both music and poetry.[2] Campion himself, however, regarded his Latin poetry as his major work and his ayres, according to Philip Rosseter, were 'these light fruits as superfluous blossomes of his deeper studies'.[3] Although identifiably separate, his work in differing genres should not necessarily be compartmentalised. Campion continued writing Latin poetry, English lyric poetry, and lute ayres throughout his life. And his approach to each of these kinds interacts. He says, for example, that his lute ayres are influenced by the type of poetry he wrote, which in turn is fashioned by examples from classical verse:

> What Epigrams are in Poetrie, the same are Ayres in musicke, then in their chiefe perfection when they are short and well seasoned ... And as *Martiall* speaks in defence of his short Epigrams, so may I say in th'apologie of Ayres, that where there is a full volume, there can be no imputation of shortnes. The Lyricke Poets among the Greekes, and Latines were first inuenters of Ayres, tying themselues strictly to the number, and value of their sillables ... Ayres haue both their Art and pleasure, and I will conclude of them as the Poet did in his censure, of *Catvllvs* the Lyricke, and *Vergil* the Heroicke writer:
>
>> Tantum magna suo debet Verona Catullo:
>> Quantum parua suo Mantua Vergilio.[4]

The generic interaction between music, poetry and classical verse is apparent in much of Campion's commentary. The prefaces to several of his books of ayres contain provocative statements on the nature of the English ayre, approaches to word-setting and elements of prosodic theory. Evidence that Campion was a polemicist as well as a 'maker' is clear, here and elsewhere. His concepts of prosodic theory are developed in his *Observations in the Art of English Poesie* (1602), where he advocates experimenting with new rhythms in English verse derived from an understanding of Latin scansion coupled with a perception of musical rhythm which, though not explicitly stated, must be taken into account when considering the application of his theory to practice.[5] Similarly, Campion complements his compositional practice with a music treatise. The bass–treble orientation of his ayres and their simple triadic harmony are the

fundamental principles behind the thinking in *A New Way of Making ...
Counterpoint*.

It is surprising that Campion should have published so much theory, generally
the remit of professional musicians and poets during the sixteenth and seventeenth centuries, though by no means exclusively so. There is little or no evidence
that Campion was a professional musician or poet. In contrast to most of his lutenist contemporaries and friends, notably John Dowland[6] and Philip Rosseter,[7] he
did not earn his living exclusively by playing,[8] writing or teaching music; nor by
writing poetry for the theatre, publication or noble patronage. Campion's only
professional training seems to have been as a physician, later in his life.[9]

That Campion's music theory should appear to owe more to German than to
Italian theory is significant. It is more than mere coincidence that the
madrigalists, notably Thomas Morley, should turn to Italian theory, particularly
to Zarlino, and the lutenists, Campion and Dowland, should prefer German.
Whilst Morley was not exclusively a composer of madrigals – he published a
book of ayres in 1600 – his primary interest was the madrigal. Campion, on the
other hand, makes it clear that he does not regard the madrigal as a suitable
genre for setting words because in his opinion polyphony detracts from the
clarity of expression and the form of the poem:

> But there are some [madrigalists], who to appear the more deepe, and singular in
> their iudgement, will admit no Musicke but that which is long, intricate, bated with
> fuge, chained with sincopation, and where the nature of euerie word is precisely
> exprest in the Note ... But such childish obseruing of words is altogether ridicu-
> lous, and we ought to maintaine as well in Notes, as in action a manly cariage,
> gracing no word, but that which is eminent, and emphaticall. (Preface 'To The
> Reader' in *A Booke of Ayres*, 1601)

Campion acknowledges a debt to Calvisius in his treatise but, as we shall see, he
relates, probably by coincidence, more to contemporary German thinking, to
Burmeister and other disciples of Calvisius. Morley's *A Plaine and Easie Intro-
duction to Practicall Musicke* (1597) is dependent directly on Zarlino. Whilst
Dowland contributes little to early seventeenth-century theory, his translation
of the 'Micrologus' of Ornithoparcus is a translation of a treatise emanating
from Germany, not Italy. Andreas Ornithoparcus (or Ornitoparchus, or
Vogelsang, or Vogelgesang) was born in Meiningen *c*.1485 and died at
Münster *c*.1536. The *Musice active micrologus* was first printed in Leipzig in
January 1517. An exposition of late fifteenth- and early sixteenth-century
discussion of musical practice, it was outmoded by Dowland's day and is of
little relevance to our discussion. But, taken in context, it seems to reinforce the
philosophical and theoretical division between the English madrigalists and
lutenists, exemplified by Morley on one side and Campion on the other. The
madrigalists are traditional and owe allegiance to Italian Renaissance music
and theory; the lutenists are modern (Dowland's translation of an outdated treatise notwithstanding) and turn to German theory as a manifestation of that

modernity – paradoxically, since the new music at the beginning of the seventeenth century stemmed from Italy. It is perhaps relevant that German theory was written in Latin, and therefore accessible to educated Englishmen, perhaps more so than Italian.

Whilst the historical significance or place of Campion's treatise can be adjudged, its practical or pedagogical purpose is harder to define. A reading of the treatise from a retrospective advantage point reveals progressive ideas concerning the latent theory of inversions, the fundamental bass, cadences and tonality, and the major–minor octave scale. But explanations for these new (Baroque) theories are not provided by Campion, nor does he take the reader through the necessary procedures for understanding his observations. Why, for example, in the key of G (major) do the bass notes A, B, E and F♯ call for sixth chords, except as Campion equivocally asserts, that they 'want due latitude', which may indicate that they lack sufficient distance from the other voices or parts? However, that presupposes what the other parts are, which is not discoverable except from the point of view of the bass. This is a particular instance of an oddity that permeates the treatise, namely that the harmony is derived from the bass, even though the bass line is not a 'given' in most of the music of his own day, least of all his own, and we are not told how to generate a bass from a melody. Yet he does give all the information needed on the assumption that chords of the sixth are to be used. A later passage in the treatise deals with the situation where the outer parts move in parallel thirds and their compounds, itself an exception to his rule; and where one of the chords has an F♯ in the bass this in turn entails further manipulation of the inner parts, contrary to his rules previously given. He has not described the 'function' of the 6/3 chord at this point (below, p. 56) any more coherently than he had done before.

Campion's descriptions of the cadences to be taken in relative keys are also radical but unexplained. These cadence points were to become the norms for Baroque key progressions, but were not part of Renaissance tonal language. They were, however, to be found in certain contemporary sources, notably lute songs (including Campion's own) and keyboard music. The planned tonal scheme of the quasi-pedagogical work *Parthenia* (1612/13) accords with Campion's closes.[10] The book is in the 'key' of G. The tonal scheme follows Campion's 'proper' closes in the subdominant, supertonic and dominant. It is unlikely that theory, preceding practice, led to this pattern and more probable that Campion's theory was derived from practice. This would help explain why so little reasoning is provided in a treatise which is extraordinarily 'correct' and progressive in its observations.

The importance of later sixteenth- and early seventeenth-century English music theory has largely been underestimated or, sometimes, ignored by twentieth-century commentators writing about contemporary English musical practice. Those critics have mainly preferred, it would seem, to discuss English music in the light of Continental or 'forain' theory. The problem is, as Jessie Ann Owens sees it,

> that none of these approaches employs concepts derived from theoretical writings that originated at approximately the same time and in the same geographical area as the music itself. Byrd surely did not employ the kind of modality we associate with Lasso or Palestrina, and still less either the modern version – 'neo-modality' – or tonality. I believe that close reading of contemporary English theory can provide some of the elements on which a historically grounded critical approach could be based.[11]

English theoretical writings, Owens affirms, can be divided into three main categories:

> The first ... consists of published – or manuscript – treatises about 'practicall musicke', whose aim is to teach the art of singing (the notes and their names, notation of pitch and rhythm, solmisation) and elementary counterpoint (often referred to as 'descant'). A second category consists of psalm books ... some of [which] contain brief anonymous prefaces or instructions to aid the musically illiterate reader ... A third category, which like the second was directed towards the musical amateurs, consists of instrumental tutors.[12]

The surviving published treatises[13] in the first category are: William Bathe, *A Brief Introduction to the True Arte of Musicke* (1584) and his *A Briefe Introduction to the Skill of Song* (c.1592); anonymous, *The Pathway to Musicke* (1596); Thomas Morley, *A Plaine and Easie Introduction to Practicall Musicke* (1597); Thomas Campion, *A New Way of Making Fowre Parts in Counterpoint* (c.1614); Thomas Ravenscroft, *A Briefe Discourse of the True (but Neglected) Use of Charact'ring the Degrees ... in Measurable Musicke* (1614); Elway Bevin, *A Brief and Short Instruction of the Art of Musicke* (1631); and Charles Butler, *The Principles of Musik* (1636). There are two important unpublished treatises from the early seventeenth century, namely Ravenscroft's *Treatise of Musicke* (c.1610) and John Coprario's *Rules how to Compose* (c.1610).

All these treatises, with the exceptions of Bevin's and of Ravenscroft's manuscript, have been published in modern editions.[14] There is, however, no accurate or reliable modern edition of Campion's treatise, perhaps the most enigmatic of the group, but nonetheless indispensable.

Date of Treatise

Campion's treatise was 'Printed by T[homas] S[nodham] for Iohn Browne, and ... sold at his shop in Saint Dunstanes Church-yard, in Fleetstreet' some time in the second decade of the seventeenth century, but it is undated (see Fig. 1).[15] Such an approximate date might suffice were it not for the fact that the significance of Campion's treatise is complicated by its close relationship to Coprario's *Rules how to Compose,* and the interdependency of the two treatises. It is important, therefore, that a more precise date for Campion's treatise be determined.

The title page does not afford any clues as to precise dating. It is among one of the very few of Snodham's 'plain' title pages and does not use the border fleurons which might have helped in its dating.[16] Campion's treatise is dedicated 'To the Flowre of Princes, Charles, Prince of Great Brittaine' and in the dedicatory epistle he is called 'most sacred Prince' and 'most mighty Prince'. Prince Charles became the Prince of Wales on 4 November 1616 and would have been addressed by that title in any printed dedication. That he is not provides an end date for this publication. Moreover, in the third chapter of his treatise Campion refers to Calvisius in the present tense. Calvisius died on 24 November 1615. Campion may or may not have known this, but in any case Vivian's date of around 1617 (*Works*, p. xlvi) is not acceptable.

In view of Campion's connection with King James's firstborn and Prince Henry's musical and literary circles,[17] and in the light of the sentiments expressed in the *Songs of Mourning*, referring to Prince Henry:

> The Prince of men, the Prince of all that bore
> Ever that princely name.
> (*An Elegie*, 13–14)

it would seem highly improbable that Campion should dedicate his treatise to Prince Charles before Prince Henry's premature death on 6 November 1612, or indeed before the *Songs of Mourning* were published in 1613. Moreover, the last song in *Two Bookes of Ayres. The First* (undated but not released before 1613) contains an elegy on Prince Henry, beginning:

> All lookes be pale, harts cold as stone,
> For *Hally* now is dead, and gone,
>   *Hally*, in whose sight,
>   Most sweet sight,
>   All the earth late tooke delight.
> Eu'ry eye, weepe with mee.
> Ioyes drown'd in teares must be.

Another ayre in the same book, 'Bravely deckt, come forth, bright day' (*Two Bookes* I, vi), addressed to the king and commemorating the discovery of the so-called Gunpowder Plot (1605), also contains a reference to Charles in terms that would not have been appropriate prior to Henry's death:

> May blest *Charles*, thy comfort be,
>   Firmer then his Brother:
> May his heart the loue of peace and wisedome
>   learne from thee.

A NEVV VVAY
OF MAKING FOWRE

parts in *Counter-point*, by a
moſt familiar, and infallible
RVLE.

Secondly, a neceſſary diſcourſe of *Keyes*,
and their proper *Cloſes*.

Thirdly, the allowed paſſages of all *Concords*
perfect, or imperfect, are declared.

Alſo by way of Preface, *the nature of the Scale is
expreſſed, with a briefe Method teaching to Sing.*

By THO: CAMPION.

LONDON:
Printed by *T. S.* for *Iohn Browne*, and are to be
ſold at his ſhop in Saint *Dunſtanes* Church-yard,
in Fleetſtreet.

Figure 1 Title page (sig. A1)

There is no reason to suppose the unique extant edition of this treatise is a second or later edition with a changed dedication, so 1613 must be the earliest acceptable date of publication.

Other than the dedication there is no hard evidence to help determine the date of publication. 1613 is possible. That year certainly saw the publication of *Songs of Mourning*, also printed for John Browne of St Dunstan's Churchyard, and the Description of the Entertainment at 'Cawsome House' (i.e., Caversham House, near Reading), printed some time after April (the date of the Entertainment for Queen Anne) together with the Description of the *Lords Masque*, presented at Whitehall in February 1613 to celebrate the marriage of Frederic, Count Palatine and Princess Elizabeth. Campion's *Two Bookes of Ayres* may well have been issued in 1613 or early 1614. The elegy on Prince Henry and the fact that it was printed by Thomas Snodham for Matthew Lownes[18] and John Browne help locate a date for this publication. Towards the end of 1613 Campion must have been busy preparing the masque for the celebration of the marriage of the Earl of Somerset and the Lady Frances Howard, presented at Whitehall on 26 December, and published in 1614.

The inclusion, as examples, in the treatise of several ayres from the third and fourth books may be significant. It would be reasonable to suppose that Campion would not publish ayres from his last books, even though they may have been composed some time earlier, before he had issued his first two books. The third and fourth books were published together, most probably in 1617 or 1618. This would suggest therefore that the treatise came out some time between the two publications.

In the opening paragraph of his first chapter, 'Of Counterpoint', Campion alludes to the Four Elements in describing symbolically the nature of the four parts or voices 'of Musicke': 'the Base expresseth the true nature of the earth … The Tenor is likened to the water, the Meane to the Aire, and the Treble to the Fire'. It may, of course, be purely coincidental, but it is interesting to note that these symbolic references occur in the *Somerset Masque*:[19] 'After them … came the foure Elements: *Earth*, … *Water*, … *Ayre*, … *Fire*, …'. All this evidence, factual and tenuous, points to a compilation and/or publication date of 1614.

Campion and Coprario

Between 1612 and 1614, Campion enjoyed a close working relationship with John Coprario. Not only did Coprario set Campion's *Songs of Mourning* for voice and lute or (lyra) viol, he also composed songs and music for the *Lords Masque* and the *Somerset Masque*. Campion and Coprario were near contemporaries; Campion was probably a few years older (Coprario is thought to have been born *c.*1570) and predeceased him by six years. Both had connections with Gray's Inn and could easily have encountered each other on various occasions prior to their collaboration. Campion's involvement with the court masque began with the *Lord Hayes* masque of 1607. Coprario seems to have entered courtly musical circles in the same year, as records show him being paid £12 for composing songs for a banquet held for the king by the Merchant Taylors' Company on 16 July 1607.[20] The previous year he had published his *Funeral Teares* on the death of Charles Blount, Earl of Devonshire.[21]

Coprario is best known for his instrumental music, particularly for the viol. He not only played and composed music for the viol, he also taught the instrument. It appears that he came to hold a prominent position in the Prince of Wales's household towards 1620 and he may well have taught the royal children some time earlier. Certainly, his numerous instrumental works contain pedagogical pieces, written so that his pupils (including Prince Charles and William Lawes) could take part. In this context it is not difficult to understand why Coprario produced a clear and practical guide on elementary counterpoint, his *Rules how to Compose*.

Coprario's treatise survives in a unique holograph manuscript in the Huntington Library in San Marino, California (EL 6863). It is almost certain it was not published in the early seventeenth century. The manuscript must have been completed before 1617 since the signature 'J. Bridgewater' is added to the title page. The owner of the manuscript, John Egerton, became the first Earl of Bridgewater in 1617. Manfred Bukofzer notes[22] that the watermarks of the paper can be dated between 1594 and 1614, and offers a compilation date of *c.*1610.

The treatise is now more accessible in a fine, original-size facsimile edition, edited with an introduction by Manfred Bukofzer (Los Angeles, 1952). The manuscript consists of forty unnumbered folios and divides according to contents into five sections, which Bukofzer summarises (p. 4) as:

I. Intervals and Melodic Progressions (fols. 1^v–4)
II. Harmonic Progressions (fols. 4^v–11)
    a. Root Progressions
    b. Chords of the Sixth
III. Diminution or Division of Parts (fols. 11^v–18)
    a. In one part
    b. In the bass (four parts)
IV. Suspensions (fols. 18^v–36)
    a. On a rising bass
    b. On a falling bass
    c. Special Suspensions
    d. Syncopation
V. Imitation (fols. 36^v–40)
    a. With overlap
    b. Without overlap
    c. With countersubjects

There are significant internal similarities and other parallels between Coprario's *Rules* and Campion's *New Way*, which, given the circumstances of their collaboration in other musical events, seem unlikely to be accidental. Campion does not acknowledge any debt to Coprario in his treatise, possibly because Coprario's treatise had not been published or because his own treatise was written and published first. Campion does refer to his indebtedness to Calvisius (see later). Campion's omission may or may not be significant as regards dating, but the interdependence is unequivocal.

The parallels occur mainly between the first section of Campion's treatise, 'Of Counterpoint', and the first three parts of Coprario's *Rules*. In one case, Campion condenses Coprario's explanation of the rule of the division of the descending bass. Coprario's:

> If the Bass fall a fifte in devision, and com nott unto a close, you must use in the rest of parts to sett unto the first note of the Bass untill he com to his fift note, and if the Bass descend foure crocchetts you maie use in the rest of parts a semibreve, if quavers then a minim, or elss if the Bass fall a 5 in devision lett the part which uses the 5 unto the first note use the 8 unto the third note of the Bass. (fols. 16ᵛ–17)

becomes:

> it is to be obserued that in composing of the Base, you may breake it at your plea-sure, without altering any of the other parts. (p. 54)

and Campion gives an example which neatly incorporates Coprario's rule (p. 54).

Campion's discussion of 'closes' or cadences is directly related to Coprario's. The two are essentially the same, although individual words are changed in the descriptions and the order of examples is different. Coprario states:

> The Bass meanes to make a close when he rises a 5, 2, or 3, and then falls a 5, or rises a 4. Likewise if the Bass fall a 4, or 2, and then fall a 5, he meanes to use a close, then that part must hold, which in holding can use the 11, or 4 with the Bass in the next note rising, or falling, and then you must use either the 3, or 10. (fol. 4)

Campion has:

> the Base intends a close as often as it riseth a fift, third or second, and then immedi-ately either falls a fift, or riseth a fourth. In like manner if the Base falls a fourth or second: and after falls a fift, the Base insinuates a close, and in all these cases the part must hold, that in holding can vse the fourth or eleauenth, and so passe eyther into the third or tenth. (p. 56)

Coprario's first five examples are also found in Campion's treatise in a different order, each one prefaced by a 'simple', unornamented version. Both writers seem to emphasise the importance of the bass in forming cadences. This is a vital shift in emphasis from earlier theorists, notably Thomas Morley, who in describing similar cadences persists in advocating linear progression effected by the 'tenor' or melody voice.[23]

The examples of the cadences given by Campion and Coprario are those typical in contemporary lute songs. Interestingly, however, the two parts they give do not incorporate the usual descending contour at cadences of the vocal line of the song, but represent a putative instrumental contribution. It is possible that this indicates the priority or pre-eminence of the predominantly instrumental composer, Coprario. If this was the case, then it was Campion who borrowed from Coprario, 'improved' upon his prose, and simplified (here and elsewhere) the examples.

Another case of Campion reproducing Coprario's examples but changing the explication occurs when both writers advise against falling from the octave to the sixth in parallel motion. Coprario writes:

> Neither is it good to fall with the Bass from an 8 unto a 12 … likewise you maie doe well in shunning to fall with the Bass from an 8 unto a 6. (fol. 3ᵛ)

Campion intensifies Coprario's general rule when he says:

> Note here that it is not good to fall with the Base, being sharpe in *F*. from an eight vnto a sixt. (p. 65)

Campion duplicates Coprario's last two examples but adds a significant qualification in opposing such progression only when the bass (F) is sharp. It seems unlikely that Coprario would have omitted this clause had he derived his point from Campion.

Both Campion and Coprario advise working counterpoint from the bass, Campion much more so than Coprario. This principle clearly links the two works and differentiates them from earlier Renaissance treatises. It is also the most important point replicated in later seventeenth-century versions of Campion's treatise, notably by Christopher Simpson (see below).

Campion's Treatise after 1620

There is clear evidence that Campion's treatise continued to be read and regarded as an important contribution to music theory for most of the seventeenth century. In 1660, Playford acknowledged this when he wrote, 'This Little Book of Dr. Thomas Campions (for the Excelency and Compendious Method it bears in the Rules of Descant, or Composing Musick into Parts) hath found so General acceptance, that two Impressions of It have been brought up already; which doth encourage me once more to publish it to the World.'[24] Campion's book was reprinted several times in different guises, and elements of it found their way into treatises by other authors, sadly unattributed.

Several passages in Butler's treatise of 1636 are highly reminiscent of Campion. This scholarly 'Oxford' treatise is dedicated to King Charles and is intended to educate 'yuthe and children', although it is far from being simple and easy to read. It was published when Butler was in his seventies, although it is probable it was compiled much earlier over a period of time.[25] It is a mixture of the conservative, indebted to Morley and citing examples from Tallis, Taverner and plainchant, and the progressive, influenced by Campion and referring to the new music of Lawes, Ive, Lanier, Tomkins, etc. Butler sees the 'scale' as a hexachord, fixed by 'Mi'. Yet he prefers to call the notes of the scale not by their solmisation syllable, but 'answerable unto ðes 7 distinct Notes, ar 7 several Cliefs or keyz, called by the Names of ðe first 7 letters of ðe Alpabet' (p. 13).[26] Like Campion, he says that the intervallic progression of the scale, 'ðe Tune of Notes', is 'manifested on a Lute: were from fret to fret is but half a Tone, and from any one fret to ðe next save one is a whole Tone, or Note' (p. 22). This recalls Campion, the first theorist to refer to the lute as an aid to interpreting the scale:

> It will giue great light to the vnderstanding of the Scale, if you trye it on a Lute, or Voyall, for there you shall plainely perceiue that there goe two frets to the raising of a whole Note, and but one to a halfe Note. (p. 44)

In his annotations to 'ðe Setting of Parts', Butler states that 'ðe Base is so called, because it is ðe **basis** or foundation of ðe Song, unto wic all oðer Partes bee set' (p. 41), clearly reaffirming Campion's radical point about the 'fundamental' bass in harmony. Later on, moreover, in discussing vertical intervals he notes that they should be measured from the 'ground' or bass and cites Calvisius, one of Campion's sources. Butler's discussion of cadences invokes both Morley and Campion. He asserts 'De proper Tone of eac Song, is ðe Cloze-note of ðe Base in his Final key: wic soolde euer bee suc, as best suitet wit ðe Entrance and Progres of ðe *Subjectum*' (p. 81). Butler's definition of Tone is almost identical with Campion's, although he extends its meaning, distinguishing between 'key' and 'tone'.[27]

One of the examples Campion gives in his treatise (p. 63) is a psalm tune which he may have taken from East's *The Whole Booke of Psalmes: with Their Wonted Tunes, ... composed into foure parts ... Compiled by Sondry Authors,* published in 1592.[28] Campion 'corrects' Kirbye's setting for Psalm 10 because it is 'begun in one key and ended in another, quite contrary to nature' (p. 61). Kirbye's setting is as follows:

Most strikingly, Campion changes the opening note, F♮, to an F♯.[29] This correction is to be found in Ravenscroft's revision of East's psalter, *The Whole Booke of Psalmes* (1621):[30]

It is also found in a collection of psalms edited by William Slayter, *The Psalmes of David in 4 Languages and in 4 Prts. Set to ye Tunes of our Church* (1643). Slayter's psalter includes settings by Allison, Benet, Dowland, Kirbye, Milton, Ravenscroft, Stubbs and others. Campion's setting is assigned to Psalm 9, with translations in Greek, English and Hebrew. The only known source for this unique 'corrected' setting is the one by Campion in his music treatise.

The writer of a manuscript miscellany, London, British Library, Add. MS 4388, compiled probably during the middle of the seventeenth century, had obviously seen Campion's original treatise. He cites Campion's three examples of the scale of G, short passages from the 'foure parts of Musicke', and 'the nature of the Bass', and writes a mathematical analysis of the counterpoint chapter. He also refers briefly to small sections on the 'Tones or Moods' from Campion's third chapter.

The most important evidence of the continued 'acceptance' of Campion's treatise is to be found in several publications of the second half of the seventeenth century. The preface on the scale, 'A Preface, or a Briefe Discourse of the nature and use of the Scale, or Gam-ut, by Dr. Campion', was included in the first edition of John Playford's *A Breefe Introduction to the Skill of Musick* (1654). That preface, together with Simpson's 'A briefe Exposition of the Gamut' and the whole of the rest of the treatise, was published in Playford's enlarged second edition, *An Introduction to the Skill of Musick. In two Books.* **First**, *a brief and plain Introduction to Musick, both for singing, and for playing on the Violl. By J.P.* **Second**. *The Art of Setting or Composing of Musick in Parts, by a most familiar and easie Rule of Counterpoint. Formerly published by Dr Thos. Campion: but now reprinted with large Annotations. By Mr. Christoph. Sympson, and other Additions* (1655). The annotations in the 1655 publication are concise and do not alter anything from Campion's original. They are confined almost exclusively to the first chapter and are absent from the third. They are intended as commentary and sometimes clarification, although, given the lack of explanations in the original, they do not help much. The annotations may also have been included because, as Phillip Lord argues, by the 1650s the treatise 'was sufficiently out of date to require Simpson's explanations in the text'.[31] Simpson tells us, for example, some of the background and usage of the word 'counterpoint': 'Counterpoint ... was the old manner of Composing parts together ...' (p. 94); he makes it clear that when talking of 'compound' intervals 'is meant their Octaves, as a third and its eights, a fifth and its eights, etc.' (p. 95). In helping 'young beginners' to understand Campion's table of intervals, Simpson suggests writing, from the bass up, on a great staff[32] and gives an example (p. 104), recalling Calvisius' *In systemate pleno*:

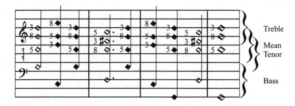

This is then transcribed into open score. Or, Simpson reassures the reader that when Campion talks about 'not true Bases' (below, p. 52), 'He doth not mean, that such Basses are bad, false, or defective, but that they have (perhaps for elegancy or variety) assumed the nature of some part for a Note or two, and so want the full latitude of a Bass in those Notes' (p. 109). In Campion's words, they are not 'formall', signifying that they are harmonic, nor melodic (i.e., equivalent to the plainsong tenor of Renaissance counterpoint), the 'true' bass being a third lower. Elsewhere, when Campion appears to contradict himself, Simpson intervenes to reassure the reader:

> When any informality doth occur, the Scholar need not tye himself to the first Rules of the Bass rising or falling, but may take such Cords as his Genius shall prompt him to ... 'Tis true, our Author did invent this Rule of the figures ... to lead the young Beginner ... but this he did to show the smoothest way, and not to tye his Scholar to keep strictly that way when a block or stone should happen to lye in it. (p. 113)

In all, Simpson regards Campion's treatise as an elementary primer; but he does not underestimate its worth or accessibility when he says 'our Author (according to his accustomed Method) doth more briefly and more perspicuously treat, then any other Author you shall meet with on the same subject' (p. 118). Simpson also incorporated ideas from Campion, albeit unacknowledged, in his own treatise of 1659, *The Division Viol or, the Art of Playing Ex tempore upon a Ground*, which appeared in a second edition in 1667 (not 1665 as originally intended). He particularly borrows points concerning the role of the bass as a fundamental or harmonic part. He further incorporates Campion's work into his popular *A Compendium of Practical Musick* (1665 and subsequent editions).[33]

Playford included versions[34] of Campion's treatise in the 1660 third edition and in nine successive editions of his *Introduction* to 1679. It was replaced in the 1683 tenth edition with a treatise by an unknown author or authors (possibly Playford himself, but drawing on material from others, which he indicates in the 1687 eleventh edition), entitled *The Art of Discant, or Composing of Musick in Parts, in a more Plain and Easie Method than any heretofore Published*. In the twelfth edition of 1694 that in turn was superseded by a new section written by Henry Purcell, reprinted in the 1697 and 1700 editions.[35]

There may also have been political reasons why Playford published Campion in the 1650s. Up to the late 1640s, he had published political tracts, culminating in *The Perfect Narrative of the Tryal of the King*. In the 1650s, he published nothing but music. Why was this an exclusively music period? Why did he suddenly cease publishing political material? Did he abandon his political stance? The answer to the last question is almost certainly no. The response to the first two is that Playford was, or had become, a royalist. The 1650s were the years of Cromwell's hegemony. Playford resumed publishing political tracts at the Restoration in 1660.[36]

It is worth noting that of the six composers selected for Playford's *Select Ayres and Dialogues* (1659/3), namely John Wilson, Charles Coleman, Henry Lawes, William Lawes, Nicholas Lanier and William Webb, all except Coleman were royalists, or could be regarded as composers with monarchist sympathies. Moreover, Playford's music book list, *A Catalogue of Musick Books sold by John Playford at his Shop in the Temple*, is exclusively, though not overtly, monarchist – books of court ayres and court composers, both living and dead.

Campion was a prominent court composer, as his masques attest. Whilst Playford stopped publishing political tracts during the 1650s, his new political voice was expressed through music. It would not have seemed inappropriate therefore that 'Dr Champian' should have been prominent in Playford's list and that the many reprints of Campion's 'Art of Composing Musick in Parts' were not done simply for artistic or pedagogical reasons.

Campion and Renaissance Theory

Campion is a self-conscious modernist. The title page firmly asserts that his is a *new* way of making counterpoint. And he is unabashed in claiming that 'might I be mine owne Iudge, I had effected more in Counterpoint, then any man before me hath euer attempted' (p. 50). Campion is certainly radical in advocating harmonic counterpoint and the fundamental bass, but his thinking is firmly rooted in Renaissance theory and practice.

The most influential treatise on sixteenth-century music theory was Zarlino's *Le istitutioni harmoniche* (Venice, 1558/1562/1573), with its companion volumes *Dimostrationi harmoniche* (Venice, 1571/1578) and *Sopplimenti musicali* (Venice, 1588), all of which are also in the collected edition of his works, *De tutte l'opere del ... G. Zarlino* (Venice, 1588–9). Zarlino's theory, emanating from his teacher, Willaert, remained in common currency throughout the sixteenth century and well into the seventeenth. His important treatise on counterpoint, *Le istitutioni harmoniche*, aimed to bring together speculative theory and the practice of composition so that the composer would know not only what he was doing but also why he was doing it. Before dealing with the technicalities of writing counterpoint, Zarlino reviews (in Part i) the philosophical, mathematical and cosmological background to music and replaces the old Greek modal system with a modern theory of consonances and tuning (in Part ii). In counterpoint, Zarlino's major contribution is the systematisation of dissonance within isochronous consonant movement and the rationalisation of the progression of inner (voice) parts.[37]

Many writers produced their own versions of Zarlino. His pupil Giovanni Maria Artusi made a shortened version in altered, tabular format, *L'arte del contraponto ridotto in tavole* (Venice, 1586). Orazio Tigrini compiled a compendium based on Zarlino which became a standard text, namely *Il compendio della musica nella quale brevemente si tratta dell'Arte del Contrapunto, diviso in quattro libri* (Venice, 1588). Sethus Calvisius' *Melopoeia sive melodiae condendae ratio, quam vulgo musicam poeticam vocant, ex veris fundamentis explicata* (Erfurt, 1592) and Johann Heinrich Alstedt's 'Elementale musicum' in *Elementale mathematicum* (1611) are both significantly dependent on Zarlino, and together with the later *De Composition-Regeln*, once erroneously thought to be by Sweelinck,[38] transmit the Italian theory to German musicians in an accessible form. A French translation was done by Jehan le Fort, *Quatre livres ou parties des Institutions harmoniques* (Paris, n.d.).[39] Other anonymous French treatises surviving only in manuscript reveal their debt to Zarlino.[40] Zarlino's work was introduced into England by Morley in *A Plaine and Easie Introduction to Practicall Musicke* (London, 1597; 2nd edn, 1608).

Although retrospective in much of its theory, Morley's pedagogical treatise was the most significant music theory publication in England to date and remained so for several years. The year before Morley's book, William Barley appended to his multi-author *A New Booke of Tabliture* 'an introduction to Prickesong, and certaine familiar rules of Descant, with other necessarie Tables plainely shewing the true use of the Scale or Gamut, and also how to set any Lesson higher or lower at your pleasure'. This inconsequential 'plain man's guide to music', quite justifiably treated with scorn by Morley, was published separately as *The Pathway to Musicke*.[41] Somewhat earlier, William Bathe (1564–1614) had written *A Briefe Introduction to the True Arte of Musicke*, printed by Abell Jeffes in 1584.[42] This was incorporated into an enlarged second book, Bathe's *A Brief Introduction to the Skill of Song*, published some time possibly in the late 1580s or more likely in the early to mid 1590s.[43] Morley's *Introduction* went into a second edition in 1608, published by Humphrey Lownes. Subsequently we come to the period of Campion's and Coprario's treatises and Thomas Ravenscroft's *A Briefe Discourse of the True (but Neglected) Use of Charact'ring the Degrees ... in Measurable Musicke* (1614).[44] Elway Bevin's treatise of 1631, *A Briefe and Short Instruction of the Art of Musicke to teach how to make Discant of all proportions that are in use ... And also to compose all sorts of Canons ... upon the Plainsong*, was described by Burney as 'useless',[45] but is not an insignificant contribution. Charles Butler's *The Principles of Musik, in Singing and Setting* of 1636 is the last 'Renaissance' treatise in England, although subsequently two intensely speculative Renaissance works to be found in England, namely Athanasius Kircher's *Musurgia universalis* (1650)[46] and Descartes's *Compendium of Music* (1653), the latter translated by Viscount Brouncker, under the pseudonym 'A Person of Honour'.[47]

Campion's Preface on the 'Scale'

The first section of Campion's treatise, on the 'true understanding of the Scale', is intended to act as an introduction, clarifying terms and simplifying the theory of the 'olde *Gam-vt*, in which there is but one Cliffe, and one Note, and yet in the same Cliffe he wil sing *re & sol*' (p. 43). All Renaissance treatises dealing with techniques of (vocal) counterpoint start with generalities concerning the scale. Campion is no exception. What he attempts is a self-conscious challenge to such treatises. His opening salvo is unequivocal:

> There is nothing doth trouble, and disgrace our Traditionall Musition more, then the ambiguity of the termes of Musicke, if he cannot rightly distinguish them, for they make him vncapable of any rationall discourse in the art hee professeth. (p. 43)

So he asks what is meant by 'Tone', what does 'Note' signify? One term can have a number of different, often interrelated meanings. These terms were first employed in medieval theory and whilst the terminology had persisted, practice had changed. Campion complains that Renaissance theorists had not updated their terminology, failing to take sufficient care to distinguish their meaning:

> In my discourse of Musicke, I haue therefore striued to be plaine in my tearmes, without nice and vnprofitable distinctions, as that is of *tonus maior*, and *tonus minor*, and such like, whereof there can be made no vse. (p. 43)

He does not, however, always fulfil his promise.

The difficulties arising from outdated terminology Campion sees as a special hindrance to the understanding of the scale and consequently to the naming of its notes. The problem occurs because the 'common Teacher ... can doe nothing without the olde *Gam-vt*'. This is a barely disguised rebuttal of Morley's explication of the inflexible and complicated hexachord system, which in turn signals Morley's dependence on Continental practice.[48] As Owens points out, Italian and German theorists in particular present the

> tonal system as the traditional gamut: a combination of the first seven letters of the alphabet ... and six hexachord syllables (*ut, re, mi, fa, sol, la*) ... On the continent, writers generally explain that the gamut is a 'universal' scale, built from all three hexachords and thus containing both B *fa* (♭) and B *mi* (♮). They divide the universal scale into two 'particular' scales. The scale with no key signature, based on the C and G hexachords, is usually referred to as *cantus durus* or *scala duralis*. The one with a B♭ signature, based on the C and F hexachords, is called *cantus mollis* or *scala mollaris*.[49]

The first point Campion makes is that the range of the (old) 'Gam' is too limited for the practical demands of music. It was reasonably satisfactory for music that remained within a limited tessitura of twenty pitches, but would not do for modern 'tonal' music. The second is that one note may have two names in the same clef. Morley introduces his 'pupil' (Philomathes) to the Gam (summarised) as follows:

1. 'begin at the lowest word Gam Ut and so go upwards to the end *still ascending ...The six notes follow in continual deduction.*'
2. 'You must get it ... forwards and backwards. Secondly, you must learn to know wherein every key standeth ... thirdly, how many clefs and how many notes every key containeth.'
3. 'Every key hath but one clef, except bFabMi.'
4. 'The syllables are the names of the notes: they are: ut, re, mi, fa, sol, la.'
5. 'You must then reckon down from the clef as though the stave were the scale of music, assigning to every space and line a several key.' (*Introduction*, 10–13)

At this stage, Morley decides the pupil is ready to start singing the scale. But the pupil encounters the very difficulties Campion wishes to avoid:

PHIL.   I can name them [the notes] right till I come to C fa ut; now whether shall I term this Fa or Ut?

Morley replies:

MA.   Take this for a general rule, that in one deduction of the six notes you can have one name but once used, although indeed (if you could keep right tune) it were no matter how you named any note; but this we use

> commonly in singing, that except it be in the lowest note of the part we never use Ut.
>
> PHIL. How then, do you never sing Ut but in Gam ut?
>
> MA. Not so, but if either Gam ut or C fa ut or F fa ut or G sol re ut be the lowest note of the part, then we may sing Ut there. (*Introduction*, 13)

But there still remains one fundamental problem. We return to Morley's dialogue:

> PHIL. Which be the three properties of singing?
>
> MA. B *quarre*, Properchant, and b *molle*.
>
> PHIL. What is b *quarre*?
>
> MA. It is a property of singing wherein Mi is always sung in b fa ♮ mi, and is always when you sing Ut in Gam ut.
>
> PHIL. What is Properchant?
>
> MA. It is a property of singing wherein you may sing either Fa or Mi in b fa ♮ mi, according as it shall be marked ♭ or thus ♮, and is when the Ut is in C fa ut.
>
> PHIL. What if there be no mark?
>
> MA. There it is supposed to be sharp, ♮.
>
> PHIL. What is b *molle*?
>
> MA. It is a property of singing wherein Fa must always be sung in b fa ♮ mi, and is when the Ut is in F fa ut. (*Introduction*, 14)

So, in the hexachord system the Mi–Fa relationship is the determining feature of solmisation. And it is this that Campion finds as an obstacle to writing scales. The hexachord takes the first six notes of the 'major' scale. If, therefore, we have b *quarre* (B♮), the hexachord starts on G, which is Ut. But if there is b *molle* (B♭), then F is Ut, even if the essential character of the scale is nearly equivalent to a tonal G minor, in which case the G is called 're', sometimes 'sol', but not 'ut'. C ut may have either a B♮ or B♭ – 'Properchant' – since Mi–Fa is not changed. William Bathe summarised this 'rule of Ut' as follows:

> There be three places, in one of which the *ut* must alwaies be: that is to say, in *G*, which is Gamut and *G sol re ut*, when there is no flat, in C, which is *C fa ut, C sol fa ut*, and *C sol fa*, when there is a flat in b mi, or b fa b mi[.] In *F*, which is *F fa ut*, when there are two flats, one in *b mi* or b fa b mi, the other in *E la mi*, or *E la*. (sig. A6ʳ)[50]

Bathe, clearly, identifies three scales – no flat, one flat, two flats – but his system does not extend to principles of tonality, or even modality.[51] His Ut is not a tonic or final. The problem which Morley eloquently avoids and which Bathe finds so difficult is when an accidental is to be introduced. He knows that in the hexachord system, the 'ut' must be changed. But this he finds unsatisfactory:

> It is graunted by the last solution, that the flat so coming should alter the *ut*, but to alter the *ut*, doth alter the key (which is the greater absurditie). (sig. A4ᵛ)

The problem is aggravated because the accidental will cause two notes to have the same name, 'fa'. All Bathe can suggest is that we allow a momentary change of 'key', provided we return soon enough to the original 'ut'.

Campion is well aware of these uncertainties and moves straight into his solution without any preliminary discourse. What he offers turns out to be an explanation of an embryonic octave major/minor scale system. He starts by saying we should not be bound by the strictures of 'Ut' and 'Re' and that we should leave them out. Thus the scale is determined not by the 'Ut' but by something else:

> The substance of all Musicke, and the true knowledge of the scale, consists in the obseruation of the halfe note, which is expressed either by *Mi Fa*, or *La Fa*, and they being knowne in their right places, the other Notes are easily applyed vnto them. (p. 44)

Campion in effect suggests a four-note scale centre, not dissimilar to the old Greek tetrachord idea. His octave comprises two conjunct tetrachords in which the semitone–tone relationship may alter, but in which the key-note remains constant.

Campion's principle has its precedents. Zarlino had already pointed out that the diatonic tetrachord may incorporate either major or minor intervals without altering its genus.[52] Morley gives a description of the Greek tetrachord in his 'Annotations' to 'The First Part',[53] but because of his fairly literal interpretation he does not see the tetrachord as part of the octave scale and is therefore reluctant to allow it to affect his hexachord thinking.

It is from this section, Morley's 'Annotations' on the 'Scale of Music' (pp. 100 ff.), that Campion's system partly emerges. Morley's 'Annotations' interpret Zarlino (chs. 72–4) and provide us with an alternative view of the Renaissance scale. This view is based on what was thought (erroneously) to be the ancient Greek system and does not have any practical application for the Renaissance composer. Morley looks at three systems, 'Diatonicum', 'Chromaticum' and 'Enharmonicum'. Each system is characterised by the position of its tones and semitones. The first, for instance, rises by two tones, a semitone, and a tone (TTST). This is equivalent to Campion's first scale. The second and third systems have no close parallel because they employ quarter tones. But the principle of melodic construction is the same: the relationship between the whole tone and lesser intervals.

The reason that Morley (and Zarlino) did not reach the same conclusion as Campion was because in their theory the 'Ut' had to remain:

> it may evidently appear that this kind of music which is usual nowadays is not fully and in every respect the ancient Diatonicum, for if you begin any four notes singing Ut, Re, Mi, Fa, you shall not find either a flat in E la mi or a sharp in F fa ut,

so that it must needs follow that it is neither just Diatonicum nor right Chromaticum. (*Introduction*, 103)

By escaping from the restrictions of the 'ut' rule and by applying what is really a misinterpretation of the tetrachord to the hexachord, Campion produces something closely prefiguring the modern octave scale species.[54] He says that the scale 'may be expressed by these foure Notes, which are *Sol, La, Mi, Fa*' (p. 44). This is his tetrachord. He then applies it to the hexachord, starting out not as Morley did with the *Prima deductio, G ut,* but with the *Quarta ut prima, G sol re ut.* Now, having deduced an octave system, this may lie in the bass, tenor, alto or treble. Campion suggests we begin with the bass, 'because all the vpper eights depend vpon the lowest eight, and are the same with it in nature' (p. 44). Because Mi–Fa or La–Fa indicate the semitones, no two notes may have the same name. Campion demonstrates this by writing three scales.

1. in the sharpe   2. the flat

   sol   la   mi   fa   sol   la   fa   sol   sol   la   fa   sol   la   mi   fa   sol

3. flat in E la mi

   la   mi   fa   sol   la   fa   sol   la

There are two simple rules: if the lower semitone ('lower half note') is Mi–Fa, the upper one will be La–Fa, and vice versa; Sol follows Fa and precedes La. The end result is that the scale itself is not so different from the hexachord. But Campion's system enables the writer to relate the various positions of the semitone to the key-note, whereas in the hexachord the semitone always occurs at Mi–Fa. The sequence of syllables changes according to the 'key' signature. The semitone may occur in three different places, namely A–Bb, D–Eb, F♯–G. Whereas the 'key-note' G is not 'altered', the position of the semitones determines 'key' or tonality (in the modern sense).

Owens argues that Campion, 'whose treatise dates from approximately the same time as Ravenscroft's, describes the same three scales as Ravenscroft and Bathe, but gives them different names. Campion is usually credited with inventing a way of solmising that uses just four syllables, but we now know that this practice was in use at least since the time of Bathe, and probably a decade earlier, to judge from the early psalm books.'[55] Campion, as Owens also points out, did not claim to have invented a new scale system.[56] The focus of his treatise is on writing four-voice 'counterpoint' in a new way based on pre-existent theory according to 'a most familiar, and infallible Rvle'. His discussion of the scale forms a preface, albeit an essential categorising one, to the treatise.

The principle of having a restricted number of syllables per note and applying them to the 'major' and 'minor' scales respectively is present in earlier sixteenth-century theory, notably Ornithoparcus (1517), Biij^{r-v} and Listenius (1549, ? = 1537), b1^v–b2^r;[57] hence also Dowland (1609). These systems, like Campion's, involve implicit mutation: Campion's semitonal 'la/fa' is in fact 'la [= mi]/fa'; his tone 'la/mi' is really 'la [= re]/mi'. Campion's solution, however, is simpler, because his descents and ascents use the same sequences of syllables, and he requires neither *ut* nor *re* since it is based on an octave scale that can be reduplicated.

Here again Campion's theory is evolutionary, not revolutionary. By rationalising earlier and near contemporary theory, readjusting certain emphases, Campion produces new theory, ahead of its time and unfortunately not fully comprehended either by its author or by the contemporary readership. But this might explain why Campion's not so simple little treatise gained so general acceptance in England as the seventeenth century progressed.

Campion's Harmonic Thinking

Campion appears to begin his first chapter, 'Of Counterpoint', in Renaissance mode, recalling Zarlino. His reference to the bass (voice) as 'the lowest part and foundation of the whole song' (p. 46) resembles Zarlino's characterisation of the bass as 'fondamento dell'harmonia', because it was not just the deepest voice of the polyphonic texture but also the foundation of the harmony (though not the basis of judging the mode). Campion quickly departs from his Renaissance antecedents when, moving into the first person singular (a feature of the third chapter, 'Of ... Concords', when he is not borrowing from Calvisius), he says:

> Hauing now demonstrated that there are in all but foure parts, and that the Base is the foundation of the other three, I assume that the true sight and iudgement of the vpper three must proceed from the lowest, which is the Base ... (p. 46)

Aware that this is radical and new, Campion qualifies his statement immediately in the next passage, recounting the historical background in language reminiscent of Morley:

> True it is that the auncient Musitions who entended their Musicke onely for the Church, tooke their sight from the Tenor, which was rather done out of necessity then any respect to the true nature of Musicke: for it was vsuall with them to haue a Tenor as a Theame, to which they were compelled to adapt their other parts: But I will plainely conuince by demonstration that contrary to some opinions, the Base containes in it both the Aire and true iudgement of the Key, expressing how any man at the first sight may view in it all the other parts in their originall essence. (p. 46)

Campion's rules of counterpoint therefore proceed from the bass and not the tenor. The melodic contour or 'formallity' of the bass[58] has to be taken into account when writing the other parts. Here Campion betrays his Renaissance origins since he seems to be transferring the idea that counterpoint is set against a (plainsong) tenor to counterpoint being 'framed' with the bass. To this end, he devises a simple table of intervals, excluding compounds (which are meant to be understood) – unlike Morley, who gives tables of compounds up to the fifteenth (for three-part counterpoint)[59] – and borrows Zarlino's extensive table 'containing the usual chords for the composition of four or more parts'.[60] Campion's table ensures that the student produces a correct progression of, in effect, root-position chords in simple note-against-note counterpoint either in similar or in contrary motion. He has silently rationalised the 'progression of parts', a theory which occupies considerable discussion in most Continental Renaissance treatises. He confines his attention to the simple, perfect consonances (the fifth and eighth) and the simple, imperfect consonance (the third). So in fact, Campion's treatise is not a new way of making counterpoint in Renaissance fashion but, more significantly, is a very early modern harmony tutor.

Campion's little arithmetic table is unique in its conciseness. No similar tables are to be found in English music treatises, and the ones in Continental treatises are far more extensive. Those in Ballard's *Traicté de musique* (Paris, 1602) seem at first sight similar but are in fact diagrammatical summaries of Zarlino's rules, and more elaborate than Campion. The tables in Burmeister's *Hypomnematum musicae poeticae ... Synopsis* (Rostock, 1599)[61] present 'root-position' and 'first-inversion' triads identified with only certain notes of the diatonic scale. The tables in his later *Musica poetica* (Rostock, 1606) are expanded, not altogether accurately, to include all the major and minor triads with the exception of E flat minor.[62]

The bass-upwards view of harmony was by no means new in the early seventeenth century, although it was not always emphasised even in what we now regard as radical theory, as Benito Rivera points out:

> With regard to the purely musical aspect of his work, Burmeister made no pretense of breaking new ground. His primary objective was to transmit generally accepted doctrine to aspiring choir directors and composers. From his vantage point, the novelty of his teaching was in its sustained interdisciplinary thrust, not in the actual musical practice it presented. If some of his observations strike us today as being forward-looking and modern, we must realise that he lived at a time when the *seconda prattica* was increasingly spreading its influence over Europe. The thorough-bass was becoming a part of established convention. His designation of the bass part as the governing principle of harmony and his technique of building triadic sonorities from the bass upward have a precedent in a treatise by Johannes Avianius, published in Erfurt in 1581, ... : *Isagoge in libros musicae poeticae ... propediem edendos* (Introduction to books of musical poetics ... soon to be published). At the beginning of his treatise, Avianius declares an important premise for his method of building harmonies: 'We call "harmonic base" that voice which at any given moment has the lowest note ... The base rules the entire

harmony and is not led by any other' [*Isagoge*, fol. A6ᵛ]. That principle finds a sufficiently recognisable echo in Burmeister's humanistically worded version: 'The letter of the lowest note will be called the conjugate base. It serves as the leader for judging which pitches can best be conjugated and which less so' [*Musica poetica*, 22]. Furthermore, the way both authors have chosen to illustrate triadic patterns built on every step of the scale ... strongly suggests that if Burmeister did not actually know of Avianius's teaching, there must have been a widely disseminated pedagogical practice that made such a coincidence possible.[63]

Discussion of key in the second chapter, 'Of the Tones', stems from Renaissance terminology but clearly depends on an understanding of embryonic tonality (major/minor) and the importance of the harmonic bass.[64] In his preface, Campion had offered one crucial definition of Tone to mean key: 'But if wee aske in what Tone is this or that song made, then by Tone we intend the key which guides and ends the whole song' (p. 43). In apparent contradiction to modal thinking, Campion asserts that cadences establish 'proper key':

> Of all things that belong to the making vp of a Musition, the most necessary and vsefull for him is the true knowledge of the Key or Moode, or Tone, for all signifie the same thing, with the closes belonging vnto it, for there is no tune that can haue any grace or sweetnesse, vnlesse it be bounded within a proper key, without running into strange keyes which haue no affinity with the aire of the song. (p. 59)

Using similar phraseology, Morley had stated that 'melody' (the 'air') and not cadences fixes 'key':

> every key hath a peculiar air proper unto itself, so that if you go into another than that wherein you begun you change the air of the song, which is as much as to wrest a thing out of his nature, making the ass leap upon his master and the spaniel bear the load. The perfect knowledge of these airs (which the antiquity termed 'Modi') was in such estimation amongst the learned as therein they placed the perfection of music ... (*Introduction*, 249)

Campion says that the key is determined by the primary triad worked out from the bass:

> The first thing to be herein considered is the eigh[t] which is equally diuided into a fourth, and a fift ... wee must haue our eye on the fift, for that onely discouers the key, and all the closes pertaining properly thereunto. (p. 59)

In other words, divide the octave into its constituent fourth and fifth:

identify the dyad of a fifth and its lower note is the key-note.

Then follows a radical statement, entirely new to English theory. Having established the key-note not by modal procedures but by the harmonic property of the bass, Campion advocates that we determine major or minor tonality by observing how the (tonic) fifth divides according to 'greater' and 'lesser' thirds and relates the bass to the tonic. Zarlino had divided the triad into major and minor thirds but not in a key-determining sense:

> The variety of harmony ... results from the position of the note that divides the fifth in a chord, or from the position of the note that forms a third or tenth above the lowest part of a chord. When it is minor, the arrangement of the chord is determined by or resembles an arithmetical proportion or mean. When it is major, the arrangement of the chord is determined by or resembles the harmonic mean. On this variety depends all the diversity and perfection of harmonies. (*Istitutioni*, iii, ch. 31, trans. Marco and Palisca, 69)

Campion sees a real distinction between major and minor harmony in practice. He deals with the minor mode first in discussing primary cadences:

> The maine and fundamentall close is in the key it selfe, the second is in the vpper Note of the fift, the third is in the vpper Note of the lowest third, if it be the lesser third, as for example, if the key be in *G*. with *B*. flat [i.e., G minor], you may close in these three places. The first close is that which maintaines the aire of the key, and must be vsed often, the second is next to be preferd, and the last, last. (p. 60)

In other words, he identifies the tonic, dominant and mediant or relative major as the natural minor mode cadence points. In the major mode, a cadence on the mediant is not desirable. Instead, Campion says we should choose either the supertonic (his preferred cadence in his ayres) or the subdominant. Then, in describing other cadences in the major mode, Campion makes it clear in contrast to other Renaissance writers that he understands there to be significant tonal differences between major and minor and that the major is not simply the minor with a raised third. No matter what key we are in, Campion is insistent that the tonic cadence and the 'rule of the fift' are crucial in determining key.

Campion's fascination with the harmonic role of the third led him to another radical observation, the identification and function of the 6/3 chord or first inversion. How Campion came to his conclusions baffled Bukofzer: 'How Campion arrived at the idea is a mystery which calls for a most careful scrutiny and re-examination of his treatise.'[65] It may be that Campion's attention was drawn to the 6/3 by applying Renaissance 'rules of the sixth' as expounded by Zarlino or Salinas[66] to the principle of the harmonic bass. Campion's rules of counterpoint had concentrated on root-position chords. He then notices 'there remaines one scruple, that is, how the sixt may take place here' (p. 51).

Campion begins by declaring how the chord of the sixth is to be used:

> Know that whensoeuer a sixt is requisite, as in *B*. or in *E*. or *A*. the key being in *Gamvt*, you may take the sixt in stead of the fift, and vse the same Cord following which you would haue taken if the former cord had beene a fift ... (p. 51)

This is a particularisation of the Renaissance generality, articulated for example by Zarlino:

> Variety of extremes, then, is found only in the fifth and third. Since harmony is a union of diverse elements, we must strive with all our might, in order to achieve perfection in harmony, to have these two consonances or their compounds sound in our compositions as much as possible. True, musicians often write the sixth in place of the fifth, and this is fine. (*Istitutioni*, iii, ch. 59, trans. Marco and Palisca, 188)

But Campion's point about when the 6/3 chord is to be taken is considerably more difficult to explain in a Renaissance context. He says that in the key of G (major), for example, if the bass be an E, B or A then a 6/3 chord may be used (here he is somewhat ambiguous, using the word 'may'). If the bass has an F♯, then the 6/3 must be employed (here he is unequivocal). The reason he gives is that 'such Bases are not true Bases' because 'the true Base is a third lower' (p. 52). This is an extraordinary statement for its time and breaks new ground because it relates the chord of the sixth to the fundamental bass, though this is not fully explained in the treatise. Indeed, it was a further century before Rameau provided the harmonic reasons in his *Traité de l'harmonie* (Paris, 1722), the third part of which was translated into English and published in 1752 as *A Treatise of Musick, Containing the Principles of Composition*.

There are, however, clues in the treatise as to how Campion arrived at his principle. The first lies in his application of generally accepted laws of counterpoint, a knowledge of which the reader is presumed to possess. He says that if the bass is sharp, then 'the eight to the Base may not be vsed' (p. 52). In other words, in this particular instance we may not double the third. Instead, as Campion tells us, we should use the 'third to the Base' (p. 52). But this assumes we already know that a 6/3 chord is to be introduced. We cannot. So we must associate this rule with one Campion describes later in the treatise.[67] Campion has already said that if, when for example the key is G, the bass is 'sharp' a first-inversion chord must be used. If the bass is 'flat' a root-position chord is needed and the normal rules of Renaissance counterpoint apply. In fact, Campion's own rules are broken, as he points out, because the third is followed by another third (to the bass) in the top part. The 6/3 therefore necessitates the modification of Campion's restricted rules of counterpoint, which he recognises and attempts to explain:

> If you call to minde the rule before deliuered concerning the sharpe Base, you shall here by helpe thereof see the right parts, though you cannot bring them vnder the rule: for if the first Note of the Base had been flat, the Meane part should haue taken that, and so haue descended to the fift; but being sharpe you take for it (according to the former obseruation) the third to the Base, and so rise vp into the fift. The Tenor that should take a fift, and so fall by degrees into a third, is heere forced by reason of the sharpe Base, for a fift to take a sixt and so leap downeward into the third. (p. 56)

Thus, the 'flat' bass

becomes

If Campion's basic rules were to be applied, the Meane should have doubled the bass, which is 'unlawful', and the Tenor would have been a fifth to the bass, which is unharmonic; or it could have been a diminished fifth, which was a sound scarcely tolerable to Renaissance (theoretical) ears. In fact, Campion's examples here are more concerned with the special case where treble and bass move in parallel thirds. This itself is an irregularity, but causes no problem in the inner parts if the bass is F♮. If it is F♯, however, a sixth note, not a fifth, is required, and the eighth cannot be used (as previously stated). The additional problem here is that, because of the parallel thirds in the outer parts, the inner parts also have to be contrary to rule. But it is only Campion's narrow rule of progression that needs modification. The tantalising thing is that Campion does not go on to explain his doctrine of first inversion. By applying his rules for consonant harmony within Renaissance laws of concords, Campion has isolated the 6/3 chord and described its presence in harmonic terms. In using the 6/3 chord, he says 'exception is to be taken against our rule of Counterpoint' (p. 52). He has effectively arrived at his conclusion by intuition rather than rational explanation.

The second clue to Campion's observations is equally empirical. The reason that 6/3 chords are to be taken when the bass in G has E and F♯ is unclear:

> two sixes are to be taken, by reason of the imperfection of the Base, wanting due latitude, the one in *E*. the other in *F*. sharpe … (p. 52)

Presumably the bass is 'imperfect' because its 'true' or fundamental notes lie a third lower. It lacks 'latitude' because there is insufficient distance between it and the other parts, or, as Simpson intimates, it is not independent: 'such Basses … have … assumed the nature of some part for a Note or two, and so want the full latitude of a Bass in those Notes' (Playford, *Introduction*, 109). Campion seems to be taking it for granted that the harmonic implication of the bass is understood. Establish the key and work out the harmony from there.

Campion and Calvisius

Campion's concern with thirds and sixths not only forms the most innovatory part of his treatise, 'Of Counterpoint', it also takes the central place in his most overtly derivative section, 'Of the taking of all Concords, perfect and imperfect'. Here he is dependent on Zarlino again, but, as he says, by way of an intermediary, the composer and theorist Sethus Calvisius (1556–1615).[68]

It is, perhaps, surprising that Campion should turn to Calvisius. Calvisius' work was not well known in England even though he was the most famous of the German theorists on the Continent, and his music is very different from Campion's. In May 1594 Calvisius became the Cantor at the Thomaskirche in Leipzig, from where most of his compositions come. Unlike Campion, he wrote mainly pedagogical works,[69] in particular the *Hymni sacri latini et germanici* à 4 (Erfurt, 1594), composed for the choir school at Schulpforta, the Latin bicinia (Leipzig, 1599) and twenty-two tricinia (Leipzig, 1603). He compiled the first Leipzig Lutheran hymn book, *Harmonia cantionum ecclesiasticarum* (Leipzig, 1597), containing 115 four-part settings in which the chorale is placed in the top voice. He also wrote several motets in which the older style of Lassus and Jacob Handl can be discerned although, in places, a more modern approach to word-setting is apparent, in keeping with the theoretical views expounded in his *Melopoeia*.

Much closer to Campion's theory are several other German treatises, published shortly before his by theorists who could be regarded as disciples of Calvisius, but who are not mentioned by Campion. All include discussion of the triad and, with one exception, consider the bass as the foundation of harmony. They also effectively identify the major and minor triad as a function of emergent tonality.[70] Joachim Burmeister (1564–1629) advocates starting composition with note-against-note harmony in four parts in both his *Hypomnematum musicae poeticae ... Synopsis* (Rostock, 1599) and *Musica poetica* (Rostock, 1606), and deduces tables of possible chords in root position and first inversion. In his *Artis musicae delineatio* (Frankfurt, 1608), Otto Siegfried Harnisch (*c.*1568–1623) goes one step further and relates inversions of the triad to the root. Johann Magirus (*c.*1550–1631) includes a section on the triad in the second edition of his *Artis musicae* (Braunschweig, 1611) which, like the title of his treatise, recalls Harnisch (the first edition of Magirus' treatise of 1596 contains no discussion of the triad). But, in keeping with Renaissance theory, Magirus calculates intervals from the tenor and does not recognise the harmonic function of the bass. In the case of Johannes Lippius (1585–1612), a pupil of Calvisius, the role of the triad is germane to much of his theory.[71] Horizontal and vertical intervallic relationships are divided into monads (linear intervals), dyads (simple two-part harmony) and triads (harmonic intervals) in both his *Disputatio musica tertia* (Wittenberg, 1610) and *Synopsis musicae novae* (Strassburg, 1612). Lippius is the first theorist to employ the term triad (*trias harmonica*). Like Campion, he identifies triads according to octave inversion and the position of the third. In the *Synopsis*, for example, he says that:

> Trias Musica ex Tribus sonis, & totidem Dyadibus Radicalibus constat ... Trias Harmonica Simplex & Recta Radix vera est Unitrisona omnis Harmoniae perfectissimae plenissimaeque quae dari in Mundo potest. (fol. F4ʳ)

> (The musical triad consists of three notes and of just as many root-position dyads ... The simple harmonic triad and true root is the real trinity of all harmony of the fullest and most perfect that is possible to exist in the world.)

Lippius' grasp of harmonic theory appears to be the most extensive and clear of all the German theorists. As Lester notes,[72] emphasising Lippius' prefiguring of Baroque harmonic theory, 'all the materials necessary for Rameau's harmonic theories are explicitly stated: the generation of *all* intervals by octave inversion, a fundamental or root form for all intervals (the fifth, third, and second), the triad as the source of consonance, and the relationship between the different inversions of the triad'.

Calvisius' music theoretical works owe a great deal to Zarlino, and include less of the pedagogical and more of the speculative than Campion or for that matter his close German successors. His treatises are:

1. *ΜΕΛΟΠΟΙΙΑ sive melodiae condendae ratio, quam vulgo musicam poeticam vocant, ex veris fundamentis extructa et explicata* (Erfurt, 1592)
2. *Compendium Musicae pro incipientibus conscriptum* (Leipzig, 1594; 1594[?]; another edn 1602; another edn 1612 entitled *Musicae artis praecepta nova et facillima*)
3. *Exercitationes Musicae duae, quarum prior est de Modis musicis recte cognoscendis, posterior de initio et progressu Musices aliisque rebus eo spectantibus* (Leipzig, 1600)
4. *Exercitatio Musica tertia de praecipuis quibusdam in arte Musica quaestionibus ... ad Hippolytum Hubmeierum* (Leipzig, 1609; another edn 1611 entitled *Exercitationes Musicae tres*).

Of these treatises, the first two – effectively the same in theoretical content though different in size[73] – are both technical, and the material recalls Zarlino (*Istitutioni harmoniche*, iii). The last two are mainly speculative, although no. 3 does contain some commentary on the musical scale.

At the beginning of his section on Concords, Campion affirms:

> Of all the latter writers in Musicke, whom I haue knowne, the best and most learned, is *Zethus Caluisius* a Germane; who out of the choisest Authors, hath drawne into a perspicuous method, the right and elegant manner of taking all Concords, perfect and imperfect, to whom I would referre our Musitions, but that his booke is scarce any where extant, and besides it is written in Latine, which language few or none of them vnderstand. I am therefore content for their sakes to become a Translator; yet so, that somewhat I wil adde; and somewhat I will alter. (p. 65)

The work to which Campion refers is ΜΕΛΟΠΟΙΙΑ (*Melopoeia*), which may denote the first edition (no. 1) or succeeding editions which were slightly enlarged and altered (no. 2).

Exactly why Campion should have chosen Calvisius is not clear. It may well have been that (Calvisius') Latin was more accessible to him than (Zarlino's) Italian, in contrast to Morley. Or it could have been a vain attempt at originality, enabling Campion to remind his readers of his classical learning, a feature of his prosody treatise on English poetry, *Observations in the Art of English Poesie* (1602). Morley had effectively introduced Zarlino into England and translated the passages he quotes directly. In his 'new' treatise, Campion would have been averse to reproducing Zarlino *à la* Morley. He obviously had access to or may have possessed a copy of a rare, foreign book – 'scarce any where extant' – which he was pleased to use. But the most likely explanation is that Thomas Ravenscroft introduced Campion to Calvisius' work, probably between 1600 and 1610. A link between the two can be inferred from Campion's laudatory verse, 'Of this Ensuing Discourse', included in Ravenscroft's *A Briefe Discourse* published in 1614, even though the content of Ravenscroft's treatise is markedly different from Campion's. Nor is it here that we find Ravenscroft's largest debt to Calvisius. In an earlier manuscript version of his treatise, BL Add. MS 19758, the debt is more explicit. This version begins with a short section on concords and discords, in which Ravenscroft states, 'Musick is an Art in which all discords ar made to agree with the concords in a sweet and well tund harmony' (fol. A1ʳ) – a commonplace notion in Renaissance imagery. He then proceeds with 'Practive [*sic*] and Speculative' music, followed by a discussion of the scale:[74] 'Musicke be directed and governed by an Index or scale' in which he refers to Calvisius: 'Calvisius doth affirm that the names of the sounds weare deriude [*sic*] from a Lattin verse which was made of St John' (fol. 5ʳ).[75] This he cites:

> Ut queant laxis Resonare fibris
> Mira gestorum Famuli tuorum
> Solve polluti Labii reatum, Sancte Ioannes.

At this point his marginal gloss gives, 'Setho Calviso Li.2. fo.121'. A discussion of intervals occupies folios 6ᵛ–8ʳ. It is only at folio 9 that the published (1614) version of the treatise begins. So here is the first specific incorporation of Calvisius in an English treatise. Although Morley mentions Calvisius once, together with Andreas Raselius,[76] and includes him in his list of authors consulted, there is no indication that he borrowed from him directly. Indeed, there is no reason why he should have done so. Morley refers straight back to Zarlino.

As we have said, Calvisius' ΜΕΛΟΠΟΙΙΑ is largely based on Zarlino's *Istitutioni*, iii. Calvisius does not have much to add. He changes the order of presentation and format, and sometimes alters the emphasis. For example, he is not as interested in 'fuge' and intricate imitative counterpoint as Zarlino; but, on the other hand, he treats double counterpoint in a more concentrated and comprehensive manner. He compresses Zarlino's eighty chapters into twenty-one of his own. Some chapters correspond quite closely, others not so closely. Calvisius' *Caput Decimum*, for example, is clearly derived from Zarlino, chapter 38, although more as an interpretation than a literal translation.

Campion is, of course, selective in what he chooses to reproduce from Calvisius. ΜΕΛΟΠΟΙΙΑ roughly divides into three sections. Chapters 1–8 deal with preliminaries – definitions, descriptions, etc. as follows:

Caput Primum.	De Nomine, Definitione et Divisione … Musicae.
Caput Secundum.	De Partibus Harmoniae.
Caput Tertium.	De Sonis.
Caput Quartum.	De Consonantiis perfectis.
Caput Quintum.	De Consonantiis imperfectis.
Caput Sextum.	De Dissonantiis per se.
Caput Septimum.	De Dissonantiis per accidens.
Caput Octavum.	De Modulatione, et Mensura Temporis.

One or two extracts from this first section find their way through into Campion's preface and first two chapters. The opening of chapter 1, 'Of Counterpoint', recalls *Caput Secundum*, 'Principales tamen tantum quatuor sunt. Bassus videlicet, Tenor, Altus, Cantus …' (sig. B7^v). In *Caput Quartum*, Calvisius mentions that consonances are to be measured from the bass, and gives a numerical diagram (sig. C5^v) and thirteen-line staff diagram, *In systemate pleno*, to aid 'young beginners'. The rules concerning simple intervals and their components in *Caput Tertium* are similar in Campion. But there is nothing specific about these oblique relationships. References in Campion, however disguised, stem from several sources, which in turn come from Zarlino, just as those in Calvisius do. Evidence that Campion used material directly from Calvisius' first eight chapters appears in chapter 3, 'Of Concords', where he cites elements from *Caput Tertium*, especially the rule, 'De Octavis idem est judicium' (sig. C2^v). Yet even here, when Campion acknowledges a debt to Calvisius, material more clearly derivative of Zarlino is mixed with it.

Calvisius' chapters 11–21, the third section, contain specific elements of composition, common to most Renaissance musical treatises, but upon which Campion hardly touches. These are:

Caput Undecimum.	De Celeritate.
Caput Duodecimum.	De Syncope. [10 rules]
Cap. Decimum Tertium.	De Clausulis.

Cap. Dec.Quartum.	'ubi formandae sint Clausulae'.
Cap. Dec.Quintum.	De Fugis.
Cap. Dec.Sextum.	De Pausis.
Cap. Dec.Septimum.	De Specialioribus quibusdam Admonitionibus.
Cap. Dec.Octavum.	De Oratione sive textu.
Cap. Dec.Nonum.	De Fugis ligatis.
Cap. Vicensimum.	De Harmonia gemina, sive tergemina.
Cap. Unum et Vicensimum.	De Harmonia illa extemporanea.

Calvisius' chapters on cadences interpret Zarlino, and are not paraphrased by Campion.[77]

The second or middle section of Calvisius' work does not stand out as anything extraordinary, either in itself or in the context of the treatise. But, for our discussion, it is noteworthy because it is from these chapters that Campion's material is specifically drawn. They are:

Caput Nonum.	De Consecutione perfectarum Consonantiarum.
Caput Decimum.	De Progressu Consonantiarum imperfectarum.

In fact, Campion simply translates most of *Caput Decimum*.

In his third chapter, Campion acts as both translator and commentator. He begins by describing the movement of perfect concords, octaves and fifths. Here he reduces and simplifies *Caput Nonum*:

> Regula Prima: Duae vel plures Consonantiae perfectae, ejusdem generis et proportionis, neque in gradibus, neque in saltibus sese sequi possunt, ut si quis duos vel plures unisonos, aut octavas, aut quintas continuare vellet. (sig. D6ᵛ)

This may be easily traced back to Zarlino. Campion has:

> The consecution of perfect concords among themselues is easie; for who knowes not that two eights or two fifts are not to be taken rising or falling together, but a fift may eyther way passe into an eight, or an eight into a fift, yet most conueniently when the one of them moues by degrees, and the other by leaps, for when both skip together the passage is lesse pleasant. (p. 65)

Indeed, Campion's 'consecution of perfect concords' is closer to Zarlino than to Calvisius, even though it is an indirect borrowing (through Calvisius). All Renaissance treatises and, of course, Campion himself say the same about forbidden parallel octaves and fifths and how to avoid them. Morley[78] and Calvisius mainly translate Zarlino, chapter 29, and differ only in the details of their examples. Campion's point clearly corresponds to these sources, but he omits examples of forbidden consecutives. Instead, he synthesises chapters 29, 35 and 36 of Zarlino and writes similar examples. In this sense, then, he is closer to Zarlino.

Campion's next point is more obviously dependent on Calvisius' *Caput Decimum*. Calvisius writes:

Regula secunda. Ex perfectis ad imperfectas facilis est transitus, tam per gradus, quam per saltus, tam ascendendo, quam descendendo, tantum voces legitimis intervallis incedant, [sig. E5ʳ] facilius enim res in pejus, quam in melius mutantur. Sic unisonus transit in tertiam minorem, majorem, et in sextam minorem, rarius in majorem. Quintus vero in sextam majorem, minorem, item in Ditonum ac Semiditonum, atque ita de octavis. [sig. E5ᵛ]

Campion provides a précis translation:

The passage also of perfect Concords into imperfect, eyther rising or falling, by degrees or leaps, is easie, and so an vnison may passe into a lesser third, or a greater third; also into the lesser sixt, but seldome into the greater sixt. A fift passeth into the greater sixt, & into the lesser sixt; as also into the greater or lesser third; and so you must iudge of their eights. (p. 65)

Calvisius' rule is a reworking of parts of Zarlino's chapter 38. He omits Zarlino's discussion of the progression of parts from an imperfect to a perfect concord. But this hardly detracts from what Calvisius has to say, because, except in one instance, the same rules apply to both. Only when a third moves to a unison, so Zarlino states, should it be a minor third. Calvisius, quite in order, allows a unison to pass into both kinds of thirds, without a caveat for the inverse rule. Campion adds nothing to Calvisius. What he does tag onto this passage is a short rule from Calvisius' *Caput tertium* concerning compounds or octaves:

for *de octauis idem est iudicium*, and therfore when you reade an vnison, or a fift, or a third, or a sixt, know that by the simple Concords, the Compounds also are meant. (p. 65)

These rules are, of course, conventional. The 'consecution' of perfect concords 'among themselves', and into imperfect concords, simply gives us a starting point for the composition of counterpoint. If we return to Campion's discussion of counterpoint, we see that he intermingles the varieties available according to these rules. This we should expect. What is exceptional is that Campion presents his argument for bass-oriented counterpoint before he describes how the individual parts should progress. So, in a sense, Campion's Renaissance-generated chapter on concords does not lead us into the construction of counterpoint; it provides us, as it were, with a means for checking whether our counterpoint is 'correct'. In effect, Campion advocates a new approach to composition, from linear thinking to vertical. And this he does not by making some sudden break with the accepted norm, but by progressing from conventional theory. Campion's ideas evolve out of his Renaissance upbringing. He does not theorise *ab initio*.

Campion echoes Zarlino's chapters 30 and 31 in his discussion of his next point, the avoidance of 'reference not harmonicall', or false relation. He summarises Zarlino by saying that a 'crosse forme … doth produce in the Musicke a strange discord' (p. 66). He does not proceed as far as Zarlino in explaining the disproportionate ratios caused by false relations; nor does he suggest when they might be permissible. This observation is in keeping with Campion's practice. None of his songs contains such relations.[79] However, it is contrary to accepted English practice, since false relations are not infrequent in all kinds of English (and Flemish) music, including Coprario's. Examples in the *Rules* (fol. 5[v]) involve very audible false relations. Coprario offers no words of caution, in contrast to Campion. 'At this place', as Bukofzer puts it, 'the composer cannot hide his English background, – in other words, Mr. Cooper speaks louder than Signor Coperario'.[80] Campion reinforces his debt to Continental theory and emphasises his progressive harmonic thinking, although it could be argued that his condemnation and avoidance of false relations, while theoretically 'pure', makes him a musical conservative, rather than a progressive. False relations may occur naturally in linear, modal counterpoint. Campion dislikes false relations because they create discords.

The remainder of his chapter on concords is mainly a translation of parts of Calvisius' *Caput Decimum*. He changes the order of several examples and omits others. He adds one passage of his own (p. 67), necessarily because he quotes a part of one of his own songs, 'A secret loue or two' from *Two Bookes of Ayres*, II.xix. He also writes his own concluding paragraph.

Campion's 'Of the lesser or imperfect third' is taken from Calvisius' *Regula quarta*, 'De Semiditono' (sig. E6[r]). 'Of the greater or perfect Third' comes from *Regula quinta*, 'De Ditono' (sig. E7[r]–8[r]). 'Of the lesser Sixt' is a translation of *Regula sexta*, 'De sexta Minore' (sigs. E8[v]–F1[r]). 'Of the greater Sixt' copies *Regula septima*, 'De sexta Majore' (sig. F1[v]–2[r]). Campion omits Calvisius' *Regula octava*, 'De usu Quartae in Sextis', which in turn derives from Zarlino, *Istitutioni*, iii, chapter 60. Campion has already given his own explanation of the first-inversion chord and, unlike Calvisius/Zarlino, does not discuss the second inversion.

Campion does not say anything new or different in his section on thirds and sixths. After a short paragraph in which he affirms the late Renaissance view that many voices in polyphony, in contrast to the transparency of two-part writing, will obscure small deviations from the rules, he finishes.

Notes

[1]   Modern texts: *Campion's Works*, ed. Percival Vivian (Oxford, 1909, repr. 1966, 1967) is a complete edition of English and Latin works without music; *The Works of Thomas Campion*, ed. W. R. Davis (New York, 1967; London, 1969) contains all the English works with selections from the Latin verse, and some music; lute songs are available in *The English Lute-Songs*, rev. edn by Thurston Dart et al. (London, 1969–); facs. edns of *Two Bookes of Ayres*, *The Third and Fourth Bookes of Ayres*, *The Lord Hayes Masque* (1607) and *The Somerset Masque* (1614) are published by the Scolar Press (Menston, 1967–73). Campion's long neoclassical epic panegyric poem on the Gunpowder Plot, *De Puluerea Coniuratione*, is available in an edition by David Lindley and Robin Sowerby (Leeds Texts and Monographs; Leeds, 1987).

[2]   Recent book studies include: David Lindley, *Thomas Campion* (Leiden, 1986); C. R. Wilson, *'Words and Notes Coupled Lovingly Together': Thomas Campion, a Critical Study* (New York, 1989); E. S. Ryding, *In Harmony Framed: Musical Humanism, Thomas Campion, and the Two Daniels* (Kirksville, Mo., 1993); W. R. Davis, *Thomas Campion* (Boston, 1987). Neoclassical studies are scarce and include: J. V. Cunningham, 'Campion and Propertius', *Philological Quarterly*, 31 (1952), 96; Catherine W. Peltz, 'Thomas Campion, an Elizabethan Neo-Classicist', *Modern Language Quarterly*, 11 (1950), 3–6; L. P. Wilkinson, 'Propertius and Thomas Campion', *London Magazine*, 7 (1967), 56–65; J. W. Binns, 'The Latin Poetry of Thomas Campion', in *The Latin Poetry of English Poets* (London, 1974), 1–25. In general, see further J. E. Phillips, *Neo-Latin Poetry of the Sixteenth and Seventeenth Centuries* (Los Angeles, 1965).

[3]   Dedicatory epistle to Sir Thomas Mounson in Rosseter/Campion, *A Booke of Ayres* (1601).

[4]   'Great Verona owes as much to her Catullus as small Mantua does to her Virgil'; Preface 'To The Reader' in *A Booke of Ayres* (1601).

[5]   See further Martha Feldman, 'In Defense of Campion: A New Look at his Ayres and *Observations*', *Journal of Musicology*, 5 (1987), 226–56; Jane K. Fenyo, 'Grammar and Music in Thomas Campion's *Observations in the Art of English Poesie*', *Studies in the Renaissance*, 17 (1970), 46–72; Wilson, *Thomas Campion*, ch. 4.

[6]   See further Diana Poulton, *John Dowland* (London, 1982), chs. 1 and 7; John Ward, 'A Dowland Miscellany', *Journal of the Lute Society of America*, 10 (1977), 5–105.

[7]   See further, E. S. Ryding, 'Collaboration between Campion and Rosseter?', *Journal of the Lute Society of America*, 19 (1986), 13–28; C. R. Wilson, review of *The Life and Works of Philip Rosseter* (1990) by John Jeffreys, in *Music & Letters*, 72 (1991), 580–81. On Dowland, Rosseter and Campion see further Wilson, *Thomas Campion*, ch. 3.i. See also K. Sparr, 'Some Unobserved Information about John Dowland, Thomas Campion, and Philip Rosseter', *The Lute*, 27 (1987), 35–7.

[8]   See Richard McGrady, 'Campion and the Lute', *Music Review*, 47 (1986–7), 1–15.

[9]   See I. A. Shapiro, 'Thomas Campion's Medical Degree', *Notes & Queries*, 117 (1957), 495. Campion was designated 'Doctor of Phisicke' on the title page of his *Discription of a Maske … in honour of the Lord Hayes* (1607).

[10] I am grateful to Janet Pollack (University of Puget Sound) for drawing my attention to this.

[11] Jessie Ann Owens, 'Concepts of Pitch in English Music Theory, c.1560–1640', in Cristle Collins Judd (ed.), *Tonal Structures in Early Music* (New York and London, 1998), 183–246, at 188.

[12] Ibid., 189.

[13] See further below, pp. 15–16.

[14] For further details see the Bibliography.

[15] Snodham started printing for Browne in 1613. See Charles Humphries and William Smith, *Music Publishing in the British Isles* (Oxford, 1970–72), 90.

[16] I am grateful to Professor John Morehen for advice on this matter concerning Snodham title pages. On Snodham see further John Morehen, 'Thomas Snodham, and the Printing of William Byrd's *Psalmes, Songs, and Sonnets* (1611)', *Transactions of the Cambridge Bibliographical Society*, 12/2 (2001), 91–131.

[17] See further *The Works of Thomas Campion*, ed. Davis, 114–15; Roy Strong, *Henry Prince of Wales* (London, 1986).

[18] On Matthew Lownes, see further John Buxton, 'On the Date of *Syr P.S. His Astrophel and Stella* … Printed for Matthew Lownes', *Bodleian Library Record*, 6/5 (1960), 614.

[19] On Campion's masques, see further David Lindley, *Thomas Campion* (Leiden: E. J. Brill, 1986), 174–234; Wilson, *Thomas Campion*, 290–366. For more general discussion of Campion and the masque, see Peter Walls, *Music in the English Courtly Masque,*

1604–1640 (Oxford: Clarendon Press, 1996); David Lindley (ed.), *The Court Masque* (Manchester: Manchester University Press, 1984).

[20] *The New Grove Dictionary of Music and Musicians*, 2nd edn, ed. Stanley Sadie (London: Macmillan, 2001), 'Coprario', vi, 408–9.

[21] For details on Coprario, see further R. Charteris, *John Coprario: A Thematic Catalogue of his Music with a Biographical Introduction* (New York, 1977).

[22] Giovanni Coperario, *Rules how to Compose*, ed. M. F. Bukofzer (Los Angeles, 1952), 2.

[23] Thomas Morley, *A Plain and Easy Introduction to Practical Music* (1597), ed. R. A. Harman (London, 1952; repr. 1963), 223 ff.

[24] John Playford, *A Brief Introduction to the Skill of Musick … The Art of Descant, or Composing Musick in Parts* (1660), 'To the Reader', 92.

[25] Revd Charles Butler (*c.*1560–1647) was an Oxford-educated man – Magdalen Hall, 1579–93, and spent most of his life as vicar of Wooton St Lawrence (1600–47). His *Principles of Musik* was published within three years of his *English Grammar, or the Institution of Letters, Syllables, and the Words in the English Tongue* (Oxford, 1633; 2nd edn 1634). Both were written in his new orthography, using substitute letters or characters. See further J. Pruett, 'Charles Butler – Musician, Grammarian, Apiarist', *Musical Quarterly*, 49 (1963), 498–509; and facs. edn with an introduction by Gilbert Reaney (New York, 1970).

[26] On Butler's idiosyncratic but progressive solmisation see Owens, 'Concepts of Pitch', 211–12.

[27] See further ibid., 225.

[28] According to Maurice Frost, *English & Scottish Psalm & Hymn Tunes, c.1543–1677* (London: SPCK, and Oxford University Press, 1953), 154, the tune is Scottish in origin. It was known in Scotland as 'Old Common' from at least 1615, and probably earlier. It first appeared in the 1564 Scottish psalter – the first complete Scottish psalter to contain all 150 psalms with tunes only. There it was set to Ps. 108. Thereafter the tune appeared in the 1575 Scottish psalter before moving to England, where it is first found in William Daman's *The Psalmes of David in English Meter with Notes of Foure Partes set unto them* (London, 1579), set to Ps. 26. Subsequent English appearances (see Frost, 155) included Daman's 1591 publications, Richard Allison's *The Psalmes of David in Meter* (1599), William Barley's *The Whole Booke of Psalmes* (*c.*1599) and Thomas Ravenscroft's *The Whole Booke of Psalmes* (1621). For a historical and bibliographical account of the psalm tune see Nicholas Temperley, 'Adventures of a Hymn Tune – 2', *Musical Times*, 112 (1971), 488–9; 'The Old Way of Singing', *Journal of the American Musicological Society*, 34 (1981); 520–23, 530–31; Temperley, *The Hymn Tune Index: A Census of English-Language Hymn Tunes in Printed Sources from 1535–1820* (Oxford: Clarendon Press, 1998).

Kirbye's setting of this tune (in East 1592) is different from later printed Scottish harmonisations, which are all very much the same. It would seem as though Kirbye was not aware of the standard Scottish settings. East/Kirbye possibly took the tune from Daman's 1579 publication. It is feasible that Campion's setting is a 'corrected' version of that found in Daman 1579, contrary to Davis's statement in *The Works*, 346 n. 17.

[29] The adoption of the initial F♯ is very odd and not something that is found at the beginning of psalm tunes. Owens reports (p. 222) that 'Temperley notes that it is the only tune in a database of over 18,000 that begins on the seventh degree'. Given that the opening F♮ is the only version in the Scottish sources, Campion appears to be somewhat overconfident when he asserts, 'This was the Authors meaning'. If the first note is altered to an F♯ then the tune must begin on a dominant chord (chord of the fifth). The F♯ cannot be the tonic chord because the fifth would be 'flat' (C♮) and the third 'flat' (A♮), resulting in a diminished chord unknown to Renaissance harmonic

thinking. Moreover, if the F♮ is retained, the harmony would necessitate a progression from a minor third to a unison, 'which is condemned'. Campion says the F has to be sharp because, as the leading note, it is crucial to the key (G minor) and is essential in the tonic cadence (V–I).

[30] The setting in Ravenscroft's *The Whole Booke of Psalmes* (1621) is remarkably similar to Campion's (including the F♯), though the upper two parts have been reversed.

[31] Christopher Simpson, *A Compendium of Practical Music in Five Parts*, ed. P. J. Lord (Oxford, 1970), p. xxxiii.

[32] This device, coincidentally, was used by Ornithoparcus and hence is to be found in Dowland's translation of 1609. Unlike Campion's, however, it refers only to two-part counterpoint.

[33] See Simpson, *A Compendium of Practical Music* (Lord edn, 1970).

[34] Including several errors which he introduced, some of which are corrected by hand in the Oxford, Bodleian Library copy of the 1660 edition, shelf mark Vet. A3.f.615 (1).

[35] For a summary bibliographical account of Playford's remarkably famous but now very rare series of publications, see anon., *Playford's Brief Introduction to the Skill of Musick. An Account with Bibliographical Notes of An Unique Collection Comprising All the Editions from 1654 to 1730. In the Possession of Messrs. Ellis, 29 New Bond Street, London, W.1.* (London, 1926).

[36] On Playford, music and politics, see further Peter Lindenbaum, 'John Playford: Music and Politics in the Interregnum', *Huntington Library Quarterly*, 64, part 1/2 (2001), 124–38.

[37] See further C. V. Palisca, introduction to *G. Zarlino: The Art of Counterpoint*, trans. G. A. Marco and C. V. Palisca (New Haven and London, 1968), pp. xiii–xxvi.

[38] See *De Composition-Regeln Herrn M. Johan Peterssen Sweling*, ed. H. Gehrmann, in Sweelinck, *Werken*, 10 (Leipzig, 1901).

[39] Paris, Bibliothèque Nationale de France, MS fr. 19101.

[40] E.g. Paris, BNF MS fr. 1361 (Bibl. S. Geneviève inv. 1081 Rés.), *Traicté de musique, contenant une théorique succinte pour méthodiquement pratiquer la composition*. On obscure French versions of Zarlino, see Michel Brenet, 'Deux traductions françaises inédites des *Institutions harmoniques* de Zarlino', *L'Année musicale*, 1 (1911), 125–44.

[41] *The Pathway to Musicke contayning sundrie familier and easie Rules for the readie and true understanding of the Scale, or Gamma ut: wherein is exactlie shewed by plaine deffinitions, the principles of this Arte, brieflie laide open by way of questions and answers, for the better instruction of the learner. Whereunto is annexed a treatise of Descant, & certaine Tables, which doth teach how to remove any song higher, or lower from one Key to another, never heretofore published* survives in one unique copy, London, British Library, K.1.c.17. It was commissioned by William Barley, 'publisher and seller of Bookes', but its author(s) remains unknown. Owens notes ('Concepts of Pitch', 234) that the anonymous author could be either Francis Cutting or Philip Rosseter, both of whom are thought to have worked as music editors for Barley's main book, *A New Booke of Tabliture* (see further J. M. Ward, 'Barley's Songs without Words', *Lute Society Journal*, 12 (1970), 5–22, at 22). For more extensive discussion of *The Pathway to Musicke* see Owens, 'Concepts of Pitch', 200 and 234; and Cooper, 'Englische Musiktheorie', 158–9.

[42] The sole surviving copy is Aberdeen, University Library MS 28 ('Andrew Melville Book').

[43] Several dates have been put forward for the publication. The book was printed by Thomas East, so 1588 must be the earliest possible date, as this was the year he commenced publishing. In 1596, East registered the book with the Stationers' Company, together with nine other books. Whilst this neither precludes nor signifies a publication date, the entry does provide a guide to publication, in this case as a means to

protect his position after Byrd's patent had ceased (see D. W. Krummel, *English Music Printing, 1553–1700* (London, 1975), 21–2). In other words, East may well have published Bathe's *Introduction* by 1596. Typographical evidence may suggest a slightly earlier date of 1592 (see further Owens, 'Concepts of Pitch', 233–4). In his introduction to the facsimile edition (1982), Bernarr Rainbow places the treatise somewhat earlier, between 1587 and 1591.

[44] See D. G. Mateer, 'A Critical Study and Transcription of "A Briefe Discourse" by Thomas Ravenscroft' (Ph.D. diss., University of London, 1970).

[45] Charles Burney, *A General History of Music*, iii (London, 1789), 328.

[46] Athanasius Kircher (1601–80), *Musurgia universalis, sive ars magna consoni et dissoni* (Rome, 1650). See further Dietrich Bartel, *Musica Poetica: Musical-Rhetorical Figures in German Baroque Music* (Lincoln, Nebr., and London: University of Nebraska Press, 1997), 106–11.

[47] René Descartes, *Compendium musicae* (Utrecht, 1650; 2nd edn 1656); English edn, London, 1653. See further B. Augst, 'Descartes's Compendium on Music', *Journal of the History of Ideas*, 26 (1965), 119–32; J. Lohmann, 'Descartes' "Compendium musicae" und die Entstehung des neuzeitlichen Bewusstseins', *Archiv für Musikwissenschaft*, 36 (1979), 81–104.

[48] *Introduction*, ed. Harman, 11.

[49] Owens, 'Concepts of Pitch', 191.

[50] *A Brief Introduction* (c.1592).

[51] For an important and insightful analysis of Bathe's theory see Owens, 'Concepts of Pitch', 192–9.

[52] *Istitutioni,* iii, cap. 75.

[53] *Introduction*, ed. Harman, 104–10.

[54] Johannes Lippius, *Synopsis musicae novae* (Strassburg, 1612), fols. H8ʳ–I4ʳ, had classified 'modes' according to major and minor triads (*naturalior* and *mollior*) related to the tonic, but did not develop his theory into the octave scale system. See further Joel Lester, 'Major-Minor Concepts and Modal Theory in Germany, 1592–1680', *Journal of the American Musicological Society*, 30 (1977), 208–53, at 222 ff.

[55] Owens, 'Concepts of Pitch', 208.

[56] Ibid.

[57] Nicolaus Listenius (c.1510–?), *Rudimenta musicae* (1533); corrected and expanded version, *Musica* (1537). All references here are to the 1549 edition, published in facsimile. Listenius' treatise became a popular primer in German and Austrian schools and ran to forty editions up to 1583. It was primarily a singing instruction book containing rules with musical examples. In addition to 'musica theoretica' and 'musica practica', Listenius refers to 'musica poetica', an early usage by which he meant instruction in composition.

[58] Morley defines 'formality' as 'to make your descant carry some form of relation to the plainsong' (*Introduction*, 149). Campion does not imply this, though his 'formall' bass, being also melodic, is slightly indebted to Morley's definition.

[59] Morley, *Introduction*, 222.

[60] Ibid., 227, derived from Zarlino, *Istitutioni*, iii, cap. 58.

[61] *Hypomnematum* (1599) and *Musica poetica* (1606), facs. edns (Kassel, 1955). See Martin Ruhnke, *Joachim Burmeister: Ein Beitrag zur Musiklehre um 1600* (Kassel, 1955).

[62] See further Joel Lester, 'Root-Position and Inverted Triads in Theory Around 1600', *Journal of the American Musicological Society*, 27 (1974), 110–19, at 113 n.12.

[63] Joachim Burmeister, *Musical Poetics*, trans. Benito Rivera (New Haven, 1993), Introduction, p. li.

[64] For a discussion of Campion's concept of 'Tone' see Owens, 'Concepts of Pitch', 220–24.

[65] Giovanni Coperario, *Rules how to Compose*, ed. Bukofzer, 19. It is probable that Bukofzer's frustration with Campion was heightened because he appears not to have known about comparable radical theory emanating from contemporary Germany, notably Burmeister and Lippius.

[66] Zarlino, *Dimostrazioni harmoniche*, proposta 40 (p. 184); Salinas, *De musica*, bk. vii (Salamanca, 1577), 63.

[67] Bukofzer found this apparent illogicality 'amateurish'.

[68] On Calvisius, see Kurt Benndorf, 'Sethus Calvisius als Musiktheoretiker' (Inaugural-Diss., University of Leipzig), published in *Vierteljahrsschrift für Musikwissenschaft*, 10 (1894), 411–70.

[69] See further O. Riemer, 'Sethus Calvisius, der Musiker und Pädagoge', *Der Musikpflege*, 3 (1932), 449.

[70] See further Lester, 'Root-Position and Inverted Triads'.

[71] For a comprehensive biography and study of Lippius, see Benito Rivera, 'Johannes Lippius and his Musical Treatises: A Study of German Musical Thought in the Early Seventeenth Century' (Ph.D. diss., Rutgers University, 1974) published as *German Music Theory in the Early Seventeenth Century* (Ann Arbor: UMI Research Press, 1980).

[72] Lester, 'Root-Position and Inverted Triads', 118.

[73] The first edition has 102 folios, and the 1602 edition of the *Compendium* has only eleven.

[74] For a discussion of Ravenscroft's manuscript 'Treatise of Musicke' see Owens, 'Concepts of Pitch', 205–8.

[75] The system devised in the eleventh century by Guido d'Arezzo, who observed that the verse of a hymn, written in the eighth century by Paulus Diaconus for the feast day of St John the Baptist, began each phrase with a note of the hexachord in ascending order. He adopted the syllables sung to these notes as the basis for his solmisation system, which lasted virtually unchanged for five centuries and more.

For the most expert and current discussion of the system as it worked in Renaissance England, see Owens, 'Concepts of Pitch', *passim*. For alternative views, and ones which the ongoing debate on solmisation theory and practice has largely discredited, see T. A. Johnson, 'Solmization in English Treatises around the Turn of the Seventeenth Century: A Break from Modal Theory', *Theoria: Historical Aspects of Music Theory*, 5 (1990–91), 42–60; see also C. G. Allaire, *The Theory of Hexachords, Solmization and the Modal System* (Musicological Studies and Documents, 24; American Institute of Musicology, 1972).

[76] *Introduction*, ed. Harman, 285.

[77] Calvisius' hierarchy of cadences in *Melopoeia* (1592) is as follows:

1. *propria* or *primaria*: modal final
2. *secundaria*: on the fifth above the final
3. *tertia*: on the third above the final
4. *peregrina*: on any other pitch

This order was modified in his later treatises.

[78] *Introduction*, ed. Harman, 142–4.

[79] In some of the part-song versions of Campion's songs (see *Musica Britannica*, vol. 54), lute and inner voice parts sometimes disagree over accidentals. This may be due to typographical error; or it may be insignificant because the lute accompaniment is not intended in a part-song performance. See further C. R. Wilson, 'Campion's Ayres "Filled with Parts" Reconsidered', *The Lute*, 23/2 (1983), 3–12.

[80] *Rules*, ed. Bukofzer, 7.

Editorial Note

This new Ashgate edition of Campion's treatise on rudiments of the scale, cadences and 'counterpoint' (in fact, mainly harmony) is not intended for the 'young beginner' (as Campion might have wished), nor for the critic of early modern English texts, but for the present-day student of music theory and history who wishes to gain easy, separate access to an important early seventeenth-century English music treatise.

Consequently, the text has been sympathetically edited according to its original presentation whilst emending obvious errors in the first printing. (Editorial additions to the text and music examples are shown in square brackets.) Original spelling, capitalisation and punctuation have been retained but the music notation has been modernised. One important reason for preserving the Elizabethan variable orthography, arguably, is that it reminds the present-day reader that 'the past is a foreign country', that words and phrases may mean something different from their meanings today. Campion's predilection for long sentences makes for a preponderance of conjunctions and often a lack of immediate clarity. The original punctuation, however, is far from being haphazard; the long sentences serve to gather related ideas into a discrete unit.

The music in the original is printed in a sort of open score with page breaks interrupting several examples (see Fig. 4). I have kept the open score, changed certain page breaks, corrected errors and have changed the clefs. The original clefs and key signatures have been shown. Campion employed the usual C (treble, alto, tenor) and F (bass) clefs.

Campion's treatise survives in four known copies, two identical copies of which reside at the British Library in London, 1042.d.33 (3) and 1042.d.36 (2). The copy 1042.d.33 (3) was 'Presented by Sir John Hawkins, May 30. 1778'. The British Library's second copy is of the same edition and also contains *A Brief Introduction to the Skill of Song* by William Bathe. Dr Hawkins's edition is preceded (bound in the same volume) by John Playford's *The Art of Setting or Composing Musick in Parts* (1660). The work is entitled:

A NEW WAY / OF MAKING FOWRE / parts in *Counter-point*, by a / most familiar, and infallible / RVLE. / Secondly, a necessary discourse of *Keyes*, / and their proper *Closes*. / Thirdly, the allowed passages of all *Concords* / perfect, or imperfect, are declared. / *Also by way of Preface, the nature of the Scale is / expressed, with a briefe Method teaching to Sing.* / By THO: CAMPION. / LONDON: / Printed by *T.S.* for *Iohn Browne*, and are to be / sold at his shop in Saint *Dunstanes* Church-yard, / in Fleetstreet. [n.d.] [Quarto].

A further copy in the Royal College of Music Library in London (L XX [917.1]) is incomplete, the last few pages provided in handwritten manuscript form by a nineteenth-century compiler.[1] The fourth copy is in the possession of the

Library of the University of Glasgow (Sp Coll B.d.66). There does not seem to have been a second edition in the early seventeenth century, but the treatise was incorporated into later seventeenth-century publications, several annotated by Christopher Simpson (see Introduction).

Snodham's first edition is divided into four main sections. I have retained these divisions and their titles, but have resisted the temptation to introduce 'chapter' heads as John Playford did in the editions of his *Introduction*, where he called the sections 'Parts'. Campion's treatise is not a unitary work but four distinct, though sometimes interrelated, essays on separate topics of music, namely counterpoint, keys and concords, plus a preface on the scale.

Simpson's brief annotations to Campion's treatise, included here as foot-notes, are taken from the third edition of Playford's *A Brief Introduction to the Skill of Musick* (1660). The annotations first appeared in the 1655 second edition, but, as Playford notes, the third edition was enlarged and included a new introductory preface (by himself?). In fact, Playford introduces minor typographical errors into Campion's text in the third edition (these were corrected by hand in the Oxford copy, Bodleian Library, Vet. A3.f.615 (1)). But the third edition is the most complete and no additions to Campion's treatise or alterations to Simpson's annotations appeared in subsequent editions (see the Introduction above).

Notes

[1]   There are a number of errors in the part supplied in manuscript. These consist mainly of differences in punctuation – a colon instead of a semicolon; a comma rather than a semicolon. There are, however, also some orthographic differences. These usually take the form of modernisations.

The same hand provides a written 'introduction' to the work which is bound in before the title page and reads:

This is the First Edition, printed circa 1616 and probably rare. It was reprinted many years afterwards in Playford's Introduction to Music.

Campion wrote 2 books of Ayres in 1610, and 2 more in 1612, in which his name is spelt Campian. According to Dr. Rimbault vide "Bill.Madrigaliana" p.xi Introduction he was buried in St Dunstans on 1 March 1619. – He was a Doctor of Medecine – see Dedication.

A few pages at the end are supplied in Manuscript.

There is a long detail of Campion's works in Haslewoods Ancient Critical essays. 1815. Vol 2. p.6.

A NEVV VVAY
OF MAKING FOWRE

parts in *Counter-point*, by a
moft familiar, and infallible
Rᴠʟᴇ.

Secondly, a neceffary difcourfe of *Keyes*,
and their proper *Clofes*.

Thirdly, the allowed paffages of all *Concords*
perfect, or imperfect, are declared.

*Alfo by way of Preface, the nature of the Scale is
expreffed, with a briefe Method teaching to Sing.*

By Tʜᴏ : Cᴀᴍᴘɪᴏɴ.

LONDON :
Printed by *T. S.* for *Iohn Browne*, and are to be
fold at his fhop in Saint *Dunstanes* Church-yard,
in Fleetftreet.

TO THE FLOWRE
OF PRINCES, CHARLES,
PRINCE OF GREAT
BRITTAINE.

The first inuentor of Musicke (most sacred Prince,)[1] was by olde records *Apollo*, a King, who, for the benefit which Mortalls receiued from his so diuine inuention, was by them made a God. *Dauid* a Prophet, and a King, excelled all men in the same excellent Art.[2] What then can more adorne the greatnesse of a Prince, then the knowledge thereof? But why should I, being by profession a Physition,[3] offer a worke of Musicke to his Highnesse? *Galene* either first, or next the first of Physitions, became so expert a Musition, [sig. B2ᵛ] that he could not containe himselfe, but needes he must apply all the proportions of Musicke to the vncertaine motions of the pulse.[4] Such far-fetcht Doctrine dare not I attempt, contenting my selfe onely with a poore, and easie inuention; yet new and certaine; by which the skill of Musicke shall be redeemed from much darknesse, wherein enuious antiquitie of purpose did inuolue it. To your gratious hands most humbly I present it, which if your Clemency will vouch-safe fauourably to behold, I haue then attained to the full estimate of all my labour. Be all your daies euer musicall (most mighty Prince) and a sweet harmony guide the euents of all your royall actions. So zealously wisheth

> *Your Highnesse*
> *most humble seruant,*
> THO: CAMPION.

THE PREFACE

There is nothing doth trouble, and disgrace our Traditionall Musition more, then the ambiguity of the termes of Musicke, if he cannot rightly distinguish them, for they make him vncapable of any rationall discourse in the art hee professeth: As if wee say a lesser Third consists of a Tone, and a Semi-tone; here by a Tone is ment a perfect Second, or as they name it a whole note: But if wee aske in what Tone is this or that song made, then by Tone we intend the key which guides and ends the whole song. Likewise the word Note *is sometimes vsed proprely, as when in respect of the forme of it, we name it a round or square Note; in regard of the place we say, a Note in rule or a Note* [sig. B3ᵛ] *in space; so for the time, we call a Briefe or Sembriefe a long Note, a Crotchet, or Quauer a short note. Sometime the word* Note *is otherwise to be vnderstood, as when it is,* signum pro signato, *the signe for the thing signified: so we say a Sharpe, or flat Note, meaning by the word Note, the sound it signifies; also we terme a Note high, or low, in respect of the sound. The word* Note *simply produced, hath yet another signification, as when we say this is a sweet Note, or the Note I like, but not the words, wee then meane by this word Note, the whole tune, putting the part for the whole: But this word* Note *with addition, is yet far otherwise to be vnderstood, as when we say a whole Note, or a halfe Note; wee meane a perfect or imperfect Second, which are not Notes, but the seuerall distances betweene two Notes, the one being double as much as the other; and although this kinde of calling them a whole and a halfe Note, came in first by abusion, yet custome hath made that speech now passable. In my discourse of Musicke, I haue therefore striued to be plaine in my tearmes, without nice and vnprofitable distinctions, as that is of* tonus maior, *and* tonus minor, *and such like, whereof there can be made no vse.*

In like manner there can be no greater hindrance to him that desires to become a Musition, then the want of the true vnderstanding of the Scale, which [sig. B4ʳ] *proceeds from the errour of the common Teacher, who can doe nothing without the olde* Gam-vt,[5] *in which there is but one Cliffe, and one Note, and yet in the same Cliffe he wil sing* re & sol. *It is most true that the first inuention of the* gam-vt *was a good inuention, but then the distance of Musicke was cancelled within the number of twenty Notes, so were the six Notes properly inuented to helpe youth in vowelling,[6] but the liberty of the latter age hath giuen Musicke more space both aboue and below, altering thereby the former naming of the Notes : the curious obseruing whereof hath bred much vnnecessary difficultie to the learner, for the Scale may be more easily and plainely exprest by foure Notes, then by sixe, which is done by leauing out* Vt *and* Re.[7]

The substance of all Musicke, and the true knowledge of the scale, consists in the obseruation of the halfe note, which is expressed either by Mi Fa, *or* La Fa, *and they being knowne in their right places, the other Notes are easily applyed vnto them.*

To illustrate this I will take the common key which we call Gam-vt, *both sharpe in* Bemi *and flat, as also flat in* Elami, *and shew how with ease they may be expressed by these foure Notes, which are* Sol, La, Mi, Fa.

I shall neede no more then one eight for all, and that I haue chosen to be in the Base, because all the [sig. B4ᵛ] *vpper eights depend vpon the lowest eight, and are the same with it in nature; then thus first in the sharpe:*

First obserue the places of the halfe Notes, which are marked with a halfe circle, and remember that if the lowest be Mi Fa, *the vpper halfe Note is* La Fa, *and contrariwise if the lowest halfe Note be* La Fa, *the vpper must be* Mi Fa.

It will giue great light to the vnderstanding of the Scale, if you trye it on a Lute, or Voyall, for there you shall plainely perceiue that there goe two frets to the raising of a whole Note, and but one to a halfe Note, as on the Lute in this manner the former eight may be expressed.[8]

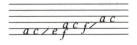

Here you may discerne that betweene A. *and* C. *and* C. *and* E. *is interposed a fret, which makes it double as much as* E. *and* F. *which is markt for the halfe Note, so the whole Note you see contains in it the space of two halfe Notes, as* A. C. *being the whole* [sig. B5ʳ] *Note, contains in it these two halfe Notes,* A. B. *and* B. C.

Now for the naming of the Notes, let this be a generall rule, aboue Fa, *euer to sing* Sol, *and to sing* Sol *euer under* La.

Here in the flat Gam-vt, *you may finde* La Fa *below, and* Mi Fa *aboue; which on the Lute take their places thus:*[9]

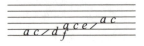

The lower halfe Note is betweene C. *and* D. *the higher betweene* E. *and* A. *but next let vs examine this Key as it is flat in* Elami, *which being properly to be set in* Are, *so is it to be sung with ease,* La *in stead of* Re, *being the right limits of this eight.*

Mi Fa *here holds his place below, and* La Fa *aboue* [sig. B5^v] *but yet remoued a Note lower: The same on the Lute.*[10]

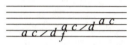

You shall here finde the vpper halfe Note placed a fret lower then it was in the example of the flat Gam-vt *which was set downe next before, by reason of the flat in* Elami, *which makes that whole Note but halfe so much as it was being sharpe.*

This is an easie way for him that would eyther with ayde of a teacher, or by his owne industrie learne to sing, and if hee shall well beare in minde the placing of the halfe Notes, it will helpe him much in the knowledge of the cords,[11] *which haue all their variety from the halfe Note.*

Of Counterpoint.

The parts of Musicke are in all but foure, howsoeuer some skilfull Musitions haue composed songs of twenty, thirty, and forty parts:[12] for be the parts neuer so many, they are but one of these foure in nature. The names of those foure parts are these. The *Base* which is the lowest part and foundation of the whole song:[13] the *Tenor*, placed next aboue the *Base*: next aboue the *Tenor* the *Meane* or *Counter-Tenor*, and in the highest place the *Treble*. These foure parts by the learned are said to resemble the foure Elements, the Base expresseth the true nature of the earth, who being the grauest and lowest of all the Elements, is as a foundation to the rest. The Tenor is likened to the water, the Meane to the Aire, and the Treble to the Fire. Moreouer, by how much the water is more light then the earth, by so much is the Aire lighter then the Water, and Fire then Aire:[14] They haue also in their natiue property euery one place aboue the other, the lighter vppermost, the waightiest in the bottome. Hauing now de-[sig. B6ᵛ] monstrated that there are in all but foure parts, and that the Base is the founda- tion of the other three, I assume that the true sight and iudgement of the vpper three must proceed from the lowest, which is the Base, and also I conclude that euery part in nature doth affect his proper and naturall place as the elements doe.[15]

True it is that the auncient Musitions who entended their Musicke onely for the Church, tooke their sight from the Tenor, which was rather done out of necessity then any respect to the true nature of Musicke: for it was vsuall with them to haue a Tenor as a Theame,[16] to which they were compelled to adapt their other parts: But I will plainely conuince by demonstration that contrary to some opinions, the Base containes in it both the Aire[17] and true iudgement of the Key, expressing how any man at the first sight may view in it all the other parts in their originall essence.

In respect of the variety in Musicke which is attained to by farther proceeding in the Arte, as when Notes are shifted out of their natiue places, the Base aboue the Tenor, or the Tenor aboue the Meane, and the Meane aboue the Treble, this kinde of Counterpoint, which I promise, may appeare simple and onely fit for young beginners (as indeede chiefly it is) yet the right speculation may giue much satisfaction, euen to the most skilfull, laying open vnto them, how manifest and certaine are the first grounds[18] of Counterpoint.

[sig. B7ʳ] First, it is in this case requisite that a formall Base[19] or at least part thereof be framed,[20] the Notes, rising and falling according to the nature of that part, not so much by degrees[21] as by leaps of a third, fourth, or fift, or eight, a sixt being seldome, a seauenth neuer vsed, and neyther of both without the discretion of a skilfull Composer. Next wee must consider whether the Base doth rise or fall, for in that consists the mistery: That rising or that falling doth neuer exceed a fourth, for a fourth aboue, is the same that a fift is vnderneath, and a fourth vnderneath is as a fift aboue, for example, if a Base shall rise thus:[22]

The first rising is said to be by degrees, because there is no Note betweene the two Notes, the second rising is by leaps, for *G.* skips ouer *A.* to *B.* and so leaps into a third, the third example also leaps two Notes into a fourth. Now for this fourth if the Base had descended from *G.* aboue to *C.* vnderneath, that descending fift in sight and vse had beene all one with the fourth, as here you may discerne, for they both begin and end in the same keys: thus.[23]

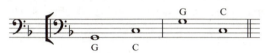

This rule likewise holds if the Notes descend a [sig. B7ᵛ] second, third or fourth; for the fift ascending, is all one with the fourth descending, example of the first Notes.

The third two Notes which make the distance of a fourth, are all one with this fift following[.]

But let vs make our approach yet neerer. If the Base shall ascend either a second, third, or fourth, that part which stands in the third or tenth aboue the Base, shall fall into an eight, that which is a fift shall passe into a third, & that which is an eight shall remoue into a fift.

But that all this may appeare more plaine and easie,[24] I haue drawne it all into these six figures.[25]

8	3	5
3	5	8

Though you finde here only mentioned and figured a third, fift and eight, yet not onely these single concords are ment, but by them also their compounds, as a tenth, a twelfth, a fifteenth, and so vpward, and also the vnison as well as the eight.[26]

This being graunted, I will giue you example of those figures prefixed: When the Base riseth, beginning [sig. B8ʳ] from the lowest figure, and rising to the vpper; as if the Base should rise a second, in this manner.

Then if you will beginne with your third, you must set your Note in *Alamire*, which is a third to *Ffavt*, and so looke vpward, and that cord which you see next above it vse, and that is an eight in *Gsolrevt*.

After that, if you will take a fift to the first Note, you must looke vpward and take the third you finde there for the second Note. Lastly if you take an eight for the first Note, you must take for the second Note the corde aboue it, which is the fift.[27]

Example of all the three parts added to the Base.

[sig. B8ᵛ] What parts arise out of the rising of the second; the same answere in the rising of the third and fourth, thus:

This riseth a third,   this riseth a fourth.

Albeit any man by the rising of parts, might of himselfe conceiue the same reason in the falling of them, yet that nothing may be thought obscure, I will also illustrate the descending Notes by example.

If the Base descends or falls, a second, third, or fourth, or riseth a fift (which is all one as if it had fallen a fourth as hath beene shewed before) then looke vpon the six figures, where in the first place you shall finde the eight which descends into the third, in the second place the third descending into the fift, and in [sig. C1ʳ] the third and last place the fift which hath vnder it an eight.

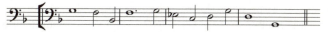

Thus much for the rising and falling of the Base in seuerall [parts]; now I will giue you a briefe example of both of them mixed together in the plainest fashion, let this straine serue for the Base.

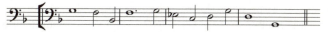

The first two Notes fall a second, the second and third Notes fall a fift, which you must call rising a forth, the third and forth Notes rise a fift which you must name the fourth falling, the fourth and fift Notes rise a second, the fift and sixt notes fall a third, [sig. C1ᵛ] the sixt and seauenth Notes also fall a third, the seauenth and eight rise a second, the eight and ninth Notes rise a fourth, the ninth and tenth fall a fourth, the tenth and eleuenth Notes fall a fift, which you must reckon rising a fourth.

Being thus prepared, you may chuse whether you will begin with an eight, a fift, or a third; for as soone as you haue taken any one of them, all the other Notes follow necessarily without respect of the rest of the parts, and euery one orderly without mixing, keeps his proper place aboue the other, as here you may easily discerne.

Let vs examine onely one of the parts, and let that be the Tenor, because it stands next to the Base. The [sig. C2ʳ] first Note in *B*. is a third to the Base, which descends to the second Note of the Base: now looke among the six figures, and when you haue found the third in the vpper place, you shall finde vnder it a fift, then take that fift which is *C*. next from *F*. to *B*. below, is a fift descending, for which say ascending, and so you shall looke for the fift in the lowest row of the figures, aboue which stands a third which is to be taken; that third stands in *D*. then from *B*. to *F*. the *Base* rises a fift, but you must say falling, because a fift rising and a fourth falling is all one, as hath beene often declared before; now a third when the *Base* falls requires a fift to follow it: But what needes farther demonstration when as he that knowes his Cords cannot but conceiue the necessitie of consequence in all these with helpe of those sixe figures?[28]

But let them that haue not proceeded so farre, take this note with them concerning the placing of the parts; if the vpper part or Treble be an eight, the Meane must take the next Cord vnder it, which is a fift, and the Tenor the next Cord vnder that which is a third. But if the Treble be a third, then the Meane must take the eight, and the Tenor the fift. Againe, if the vppermost part stands in the fift or twelfe, (for in respect of the learners ease, in the simple Concord I conclude all his compounds) then the Meane must be a tenth, and the Tenor a fift. Moreouer, all these Cords are to be seene in the Base, and such Cords as stand aboue the Notes of the Base are easily knowne, but such as in sight are found vnder it, trouble the [sig. C2ᵛ] young beginner; let him therefore know that a third vnder the Base, is a sixt aboue it, and if it be a greater third, it yeelds the lesser sixt aboue; if the lesser third, the greater sixt. A fourth vnderneath the Base is a fift aboue, and a fift vnder the Base is a fourth aboue it. A sixt beneath the Base is a third aboue, and if it be the lesser sixt, then is the third aboue the greater third, and if the greater sixt vnderneath, then is it the lesser third aboue; and thus far haue I digressed for the Schollers sake.[29]

If I should discouer no more then this already deciphered of Counter-point, wherein the natiue order of foure parts with vse of the Concords, is demonstratiuely expressed, might I be mine owne Iudge, I had effected more in Counterpoint, then any man before me hath euer attempted, but I will yet proceed a little farther. And that you may perceiue how cunning and how certaine nature is in all her operations, know that what Cords haue held good in this ascending and descending of the Base answere in the contrary by the very same rule, though not so formally as the other, yet so, that much vse is and may be made of this sort of Counter-point. To keepe the figures in your memorie, I will here place them againe, and vnder them plaine examples.

8	3	5
3	5	8

[sig. C3ʳ] In these last examples you may see what variety nature offers of her selfe; for if in the first Rule the Notes follow not in expected formality,[30] this second way being quite contrary to the other, affords vs sufficient supply: the first and last two Notes rising and falling by degrees, are not so formall as the rest, yet thus they may be mollified, by breaking[31] two of the first Notes.

[sig. C3ᵛ]

How both the waies may be mixed together, you may perceiue by this next example, wherein the blacke Notes distinguish the second way from the first.

[sig. C4ʳ]

In this example the fift and sixt Notes of the three vpper parts are after the second way, for from the fourth Note of the Base, which is in from [*sic*] *G.* and goeth to *B.* is a third rising, so that according to the first rule, the eight should passe into a fift, the fift into a third, the third into an eight: but here contrariwise the eight goes into a third, the fift into an eight, and the third into a fift; and by these Notes you may censure[32] the rest of that kinde.[33]

Though I may now seeme to haue finished all that belongs to this sort of Counterpoint, yet there remaines one scruple, that is, how the sixt way [*recte* may] take place here, which I will also declare.[34] Know that whensoeuer a sixt is requisite, as in *B.* or in *E.* or *A.* the [sig. C4ᵛ] key being in *Gamvt*, you may take the sixt in stead of the fift, and vse the same Cord following which you would haue taken if the former cord had beene a fift example.[35]

The sixt in both places (the Base rising) passes into a third, as it should haue done if the sixt had beene a fift. Moreouer if the Base shall vse a sharpe, as in *F. sharpe*; then must we take the sixt of necessity, but the eight to the Base may not be vsed, so that exception is to be taken against our rule of Counterpoint:[36] To which I answere thus, first, such Bases are not true Bases, for where a sixt is to be taken, either in *F. sharpe*, or in *E. sharpe*, or in *B.* or in *A.* the true Base is a third [sig. C5^r] lower, *F. sharpe* in *D. E.* in *C. B.* in *G. A.* in *F.* as for example.[37]

In the first Base two sixes are to be taken, by reason of the imperfection of the Base, wanting due latitude, the one in *E.* the other in *F. sharpe*, but in the second Base the sixes are remoued away and the Musicke is fuller.[38]

Neuerthelesse, if any be pleased to vse the Base sharpe, then in stead of the eight, to the Base hee may take the third to the Base, in this manner.

[sig. C5^v] Here the Treble in the third Note, when it should haue past into the sharpe eight in *F.* takes for it a third to the Base in *A.* which causeth the Base and Treble to rise two thirds, whereof we will speake hereafter.

Note also that when the Base stands in *E.* flat, and the part that is an eight to it must passe into a sharpe or greater third, that this passage from the flat to the sharpe would be vnformall; and therefore it may be thus with small alteration auoided, by remouing the latter part of the Note into the third aboue, which though it meets in vnison with the vpper part, yet it is right good, because it iumps not with the whole, but onely with the last halfe of it.

Example.[39]

[sig. C6ʳ] For the second example looke hereafter in the rule of thirds, but for the first example [look] here: if in the Meane part the third Note that is diuided, had stood still a Minum (as by rule it should) and so had past into *F*. sharpe, as it must of force be made sharpe at a close,[40] it had beene then passing vnformall.[41]

But if the same Base had beene set in the sharpe key, the rest of the parts would haue falne out formall of themselues without any helpe, as thus:

But if the third Note of the Base in *E*. flat had been put in his place of perfection, that is in *C*. a third lower then the other parts would haue answered fitly, in this manner.

[sig. C6ᵛ]

When the Base shall stand still in one key, as aboue it doth in the third Note, then the other parts may remoue at their pleasure.

Moreouer it is to be obserued that in composing of the Base, you may breake[42]
it at your pleasure, without altering any of the other parts: as for example.

[sig. C7ʳ]

One other obseruation more I will handle that doth arise out of this example,
which according to the first rule may hold thus:

[sig. C7ᵛ]

Herein are two errours, first in the second Notes of the Base and Treble,
where the third to the Base ought to haue been sharpe, secondly in the second
and third Notes of the same parts, where the third being a lesser third, holds
while the Base falls into a fift which is vnelegant, but if the vpper third had
beene the greater third, the fift had fitly followed, as you may see in the third
and fourth Notes of the Tenor and the Base.

But that scruple may be taken away by making the second Note of the Treble
sharpe, and in stead of a fift by remouing the third Note into a sixt.[43]

[sig. C8ʳ]   *Example.*

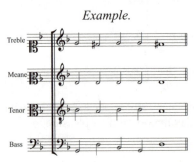

There may yet be more variety afforded the Base, by ordering the fourth Notes of the vpper parts according to the second rule, thus:

[sig. C8ᵛ]

But that I may (as neere as I can) leaue nothing vntoucht concerning this kinde of Counterpoint, let vs now consider how two thirds being taken together betweene the Treble and the Base, may stand with our Rule.[44] For sixes are not in this case to be mentioned, being distances so large that they can produce no formality: Besides the sixt is of it selfe very imperfect, being compounded of a third which is an imperfect Concord, and of a fourth which is a Discord: and this the cause is, that the sixes produce so many fourths in the inner parts. As for the third it being the least distance of any Concord, is therefore easily to be reduced[45] into good order. For if the Base and Treble doe rise together in thirds, then the first Note of the Treble is regular with the other part, but the second of it is irregular; for by rule in stead of the rising third, it [sig. D1ʳ] should fall into the eight. In like sort if the Base and Treble doe fall two thirds, the first Note of the Treble is irregular, and is to be brought into rule by being put into the eight, but the second Note is of it selfe regular. Yet whether those thirds be reduced into eights or no; you shall by supposition thereof finde out the other parts, which neuer vary from the rule but in the sharpe Base. But let mee explaine my selfe by example.

The first two Notes of the Treble are both thirds to the Base, but in the second stroke,[46] the first Note of the Treble is a third, and the second, which was before a third, is made an eight, onely to shew how you may finde out the right parts which are to be vsed when you take two thirds betweene the Treble and the Base: For according to the former rule, if the Base descends, [sig. D1ᵛ] the third then in the Treble is to passe into the eight, and the meane must first take an eight, then a fift, and the Tenor a fift, then a third, and these are also the right and proper parts if you returne the eight of the Treble into a third againe, as may appeare in the first example of the Base falling, and consequently in all the rest.

But let vs proceed yet farther, and suppose that the Base shall vse a sharpe, what is then to be done? as if thus:

If you call to minde the rule before deliuered concerning the sharpe Base, you shall here by helpe thereof see the right parts, though you cannot bring them vnder the rule: for if the first Note of the Base had been flat, the Meane part should haue taken that, and so haue descended to the fift; but being sharpe you [sig. D2ʳ] take for it (according to the former obseruation) the third to the Base, and so rise vp into the fift. The Tenor that should take a fift, and so fall by degrees into a third, is heere forced by reason of the sharpe Base, for a fift to take a sixt and so leap downeward into the third. And so much for the thirds.

Lastly in fauour of young beginners let me also adde this, that the Base intends a close as often as it riseth a fift, third or second, and then immediately either falls a fift, or riseth a fourth. In like manner if the Base falls a fourth or second: and after falls a fift, the Base insinuates a close, and in all these cases the part must hold, that in holding can vse the fourth or eleauenth, and so passe eyther into the third or tenth.[47]

[sig. D2ᵛ]

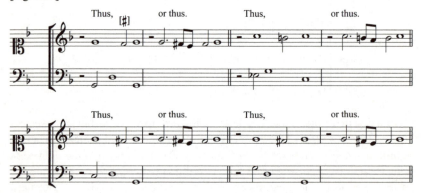

In the examples before set downe I left out the closes, of purpose that the Cords might the better appeare in their proper places, but this short admonition will direct any young beginner to helpe that want at his pleasure. And thus I end my treatise of Counterpoint both briefe and certaine, such as will open an easie way to them that without helpe of a skilfull Teacher endeauour to acquire the first grounds of this Arte.[48]

[sig. D3ʳ]

A short Hymne, Composed after this forme of counterpoint, to shew how well it will become any Diuine, *or graue* Subiect.[49]

[sig. D3ᵛ] In this Aire the last Note onely is for sweetness[50] sake, altered from the rule, in the last Note of the Treble, where the eight being a perfect Concord, and better befitting an outward part at the Close, is taken for a third, and in the Tenor in stead of the fift, that third is taken descending, for in a midddle [*sic*] part, imperfection is not so manifest as in the Treble at a close which is the perfection of a song.

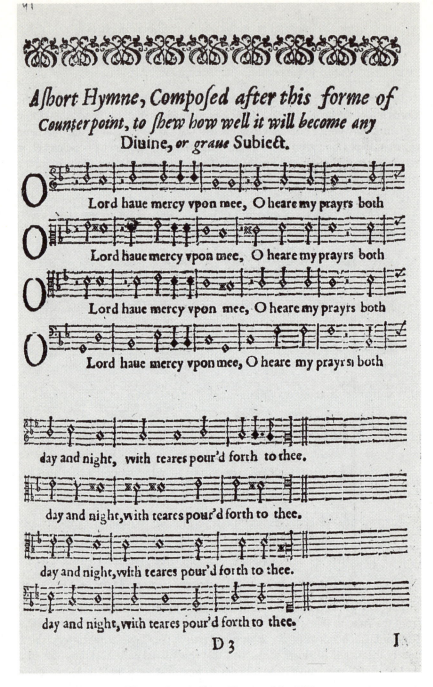

Figure 2 A Short Hymne (sig. D3)

Of the Tones of Musicke.

Of all things that belong to the making vp of a Musition, the most necessary and vsefull for him is the true knowledge of the Key or Moode, or Tone,[51] for all signifie the same thing, with the closes belonging vnto it, for there is no tune that can haue any grace or sweetnesse, vnlesse it be bounded within a proper key, without running into strange keyes which haue no affinity with the aire of the song. I haue therefore thought good in an easie and briefe discourse to endeauour to expresse that, which many in large and obscure volumes haue made fearefull to the idle Reader.

The first thing to be herein considered is the eigh[t] which is equally diuided into a fourth, and a fift as thus:[52]

[sig. D4ᵛ] Here you see the fourth in the vpper place, and the fift in the lower place, which is called *Modus authentus*:[53] but contrary thus:

This is called *Modus plagalij*,[54] but howsoeuer the fourth in the eight is placed, wee must haue our eye on the fift, for that onely discouers the key, and all the closes pertaining properly thereunto.[55] This fift is also diuided into two thirds, sometimes the lesser third hath the vpper place, and the greater third supports it below, sometimes the greater third is higher, and the lesser third rests in the lowest place, as for example:

The lowest Note of this fift, beares the name of the Key, as if the eight be from *G.* to *G.* the fift from *G.* beneath to *D.* aboue, *G.* being the lowest Note of the fift, showes that *G.* is the key, and if one should demaund in what key your song is set, you must answere in *Gamvt*, or *Gsolrevt*, that is in *G.*

If the compasse of your song shall fall out thus:

Respect not the fourth below, but looke to your fift aboue, and the lowest
Note of that fift assume for your key, which is *C*. then diuide that fift into his
two thirds, and so you shall finde out all the closes that belong to that key.[56]

The maine and fundamentall close is in the key it selfe, the second is in the
vpper Note of the fift, the third is in the vpper Note of the lowest third, if it be
the lesser third, as for example, if the key be in *G*. with *B*. flat, you may close in
these three places.[57]

The first close is that which maintaines the aire of the key, and must be vsed
often, the second is next to be preferd, and the last, last.

But if the key should be in *G*. with *B*. sharpe, then the last close being to be
made in the greater or sharpe third is vnproper, & therfore for variety sometime
the next key aboue is ioyned with it, which is *A*. and sometimes the fourth key,
which is *C*. but these changes [sig. D5ᵛ] of keyes must be done with iudgement,
yet haue I aptly closed in the vpper Note of the lowest third of the key, the key
being in *F*. and the vpper Note of the third standing in *A*. as you may perceiue in
this Aire:[58]

In this aire the first close is in the vpper note of the fift, which from *F*. is *C*.
the second close is in the vpper Note of the great third, which from *F*. is *A*.

But the last and finall close is in the key it selfe, which is *F*. as it must euer
be, wheresoeuer your key shall stand, either in *G*. or *C*. or *F*. or elsewhere, the
same rule of the fift is perpetuall, being diuided into thirds, which can be but
two waies, that is, eyther [sig. D6ʳ] when the vpper third is lesse by halfe a Note
then the lower, or when the lower third containes the half Note, which is *Mi Fa*,
or *La Fa*.[59]

If the lower third containes the halfe Note it hath it eyther aboue as *La Mi Fa*: *La Mi,* being the whole Note, and *Mi Fa* but halfe so much, that is the halfe Note; or else when the halfe Note is vnderneath as in *Mi Fa Sol*: *Mi Fa*, is the halfe Note, and *Fa Sol* is the whole Note; but whether the halfe Note be vppermost or lowermost, if the lowest third of the fift be the lesser third, that key yeelds familiarly three closes; example of the halfe Note, standing in the vpper place was shewed before, now I will set downe the other.[60]

But for the other keyes that diuide the fift, so that it hath the lesse[r] third aboue, and the greater vnderneath, they can challenge but two proper closes, one in the lowest Note of the fift which is the fundamentall key, and the other in the vppermost Note of the same wherin also you may close at pleasure. True it is that the key next aboue hath a great affinity with the right key, and may there-fore as I said before be vsed, as also the fourth key aboue the finall key.
[sig. D6ᵛ]

Examples of both in two beginnings of Songs.[61]

In the first example *A*. is mixt with *G*. and in the second *C*[.] is ioyned with *G*. as you may vnderstand by the second closes of both.

To make the key knowne is most necessary in the beginning of a song, and it is best exprest by the often vsing of his proper fift, and fourth, and thirds, rising or falling.

There is a tune ordinarily vsed, or rather abused, in our Churches, which is begun in one key and ended in another, quite contrary to nature; which errour crept in first through the ignorance of some parish Clarks, who vnderstood better how to vse the keyes of their Church-doores, then the keyes of Musicke, at which I doe not much meruaile, but that the same should passe in the [sig. D7ʳ] booke of Psalmes[62] set forth in foure parts, and authorised by so many Musitions, makes mee much amazed: This is the tune.[63]

qq

Of the Tones of Musicke.

booke of Pſalmes ſet forth in foure parts, and authori-
ſed by ſo many Muſitions, makes mee much amazed:
This is the tune.

If one ſhould requeſt me to make a Baſe to the firſt
halfe of his aire, I am perſwaded that I ought to make
it in this manner :

Now if this be the right Baſe (as without doubt it is)
what a ſtrange vnaireable change muſt the key then
make from *F.* with the firſt third ſharp to *G.* with *B.* flat.
But they haue found a ſhift for it, and beginne the
tune vpon the vpper Note of the fift, making the third
to it flat; which is as abſurd as the other: For firſt they
erre in riſing from a flat third into the vniſion, or eight,
which is condemned by the beſt Muſitions; next the
third to the fift, is the third which makes the cadence of
the key, and therefore affects to be ſharpe by nature
as indeede the authour of the aire at the firſt intended
it ſhould be. I will therefore ſo ſet it downe in foure
parts according to the former Rule of Counterpoint.

This

Figure 3   A Psalm Tune (sig. D7)

If one should request me to make a Base to the first halfe of his aire, I am perswaded that I ought to make it in this manner:[64]

Now if this be the right Base (as without doubt it is) what a strange vnaireable change must the key then make from *F.* with the first third sharp to *G.* with *B.* flat.

But they haue found a shift[65] for it, and beginne the tune vpon the vpper Note of the fift, making the third to it flat; which is as absurd as the other: For first they erre in rising from a flat third into the vnision, or eight, which is condemned by the best Musitions; next the third to the fift, is the third which makes the cadence of the key, and therefore affects to be sharpe by nature as indeede the authour of the aire at the first intended it should be. I will therefore so set it downe in foure parts according to the former Rule of Counterpoint.[66]

[sig. D7ᵛ]

[sig. D8ʳ] This was the Authors meaning, and thus it is lawfull to beginne a song in the fift,[67] so that you maintaine the aire of the song, ioyning to it the proper parts, but for such dissonant and extrauagant errors as I have iustly reprehended, I heartily wish they should be remedied, especially in deuine seruice, which is deuoted to the great authour of all harmony.[68] And briefly thus for the Tones.

Figure 4   A Psalm Tune set down in foure parts (sig. D7^v)

Of the taking of all Concords,
perfect and imperfect.

Of all the latter writers in Musicke, whom I haue knowne, the best and most learned, is *Zethus Caluisius* a Germane; who out of the choisest Authors, hath drawne into a perspicuous method, the right and elegant manner of taking all Concords, perfect and imperfect, to whom I would referre our Musitions,[69] but that his booke is scarce any where extant, and besides it is written in Latine, which language few or none of them vnderstand. I am therefore content for their sakes to become a Translator; yet so, that somewhat I wil adde; and somewhat I will alter.[70]

The consecution of perfect concords among themselues is easie; for who knowes not that two eights or two fifts are not to be taken rising or falling together,[71] but a fift may eyther way passe into an eight, or an eight into a fift, yet most conueniently when the one [sig. E1ʳ] of them moues by degrees, and the other by leaps, for when both skip together the passage is lesse pleasant: The waies by degrees are these.

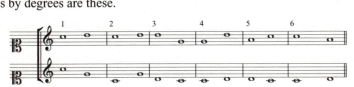

The fourth way is onely excepted against, where the fift riseth into the eight, and in few parts it cannot well be admitted, but in songs of many voices it is oftentimes necessary.[72]

The passage also of perfect Concords into imperfect, eyther rising or falling, by degrees or leaps, is easie, and so an vnison may passe into a lesser third, or a greater third; also into the lesser sixt, but seldome into the greater sixt. A fift passeth into the greater sixt, & into the lesser sixt; as also into the greater or lesser third; and so you must iudge of their eights; for *de octauis idem est iudicium*,[73] and therfore when you reade an vnison, or a fift, or a third, or a sixt, know that by the simple Concords, the Compounds also are meant.

Note here that it is not good to fall with the Base, being sharpe in *F.* from an eight vnto a sixt.

As thus.[74]

or thus.

But concerning imperfect cords, because they obserue not all one way in their passages, we will speake of them seuerally, first declaring what Relation not harmonicall doth signifie, whereof mention will be made hereafter.[75]

Relation or reference, or respect not harmonicall is *Mi* against *Fa* in a crosse forme, and it is in foure Notes, when the one being considered crosse with the other doth produce in the Musicke a strange discord.[76] Example will yeeld it more plaine.

[sig. E2ʳ]

The first Note of the vpper part is in *Elami* sharpe, which being considered, or referred to the second Note of the lower part, which is *Elami*, made flat by the cromaticke flat signe, begets a false second, which is a harsh discorde, and though these Notes sound not both together, yet in few parts they leaue an offence in the eare. The second example is the same descending, the third is from *Elami* sharpe in the first Note of the lower part, to the second note in the vpper part, it being flat by reason of the flat signe, and so betweene them they mixe in the Musicke a false fift, the same doth the fourth example, but the fift example yeelds a false fourth, and the sixt a false fift.

There are two kindes of imperfect concords, thirds or sixes, and the sixes wholy participate of the nature of the thirds; for to the lesser third which consists but of a whole Note and halfe, adde a fourth, and you haue the lesser sixt; in like manner to the greater third that consists of two whole Notes, adde a fourth, and it makes vp the greater sixt; so that all the difference is stil in the halfe note according to that only[77] saying, *Mi Et Fa sunt tota Musica.*[78] Of these foure we wil now discourse proceeding in order from the lesse[r] to the greater.

[sig. E2ᵛ]

Of the lesser or imperfect third.

The lesser third passeth into an vnison, first by degrees when both parts meete, then by leaps ascending or descending when one of the parts stand still, but when both the parts leap or fall together, the passage is not allowed.

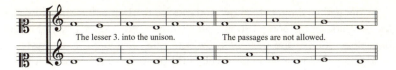

The lesser 3. into the unison.   The passages are not allowed.

Secondly, the lesser third passeth into a fift, first in degrees when they are seperated by contrary motions, then by leaps when the lower part riseth by degrees, and the vpper part descends by degrees, and thus the lesser tenth may passe into a fift. Lastly both parts leaping, the lesser third may passe into a fift, so that the vpper part doth descend by leap the distance of a lesser third. Any other way the passage of a lesser third into a fift, is disallowed.

[sig. E3^r]

Allowed.   Disallowed.

In the last disallowance, which is when the vpper part stands, and the lower part falls from a lesser third to a fift, many haue beene deceiued, their eares not finding the absurdity of it: but as this way is immusicall,[79] so is the fall of the greater third in the former manner, into a fift, passing harmonious; in so much that it is elegantly and with much grace taken in one part of a short aire foure times, whereas had the fift beene halfe so often taken with the lesser third falling, it would haue yeelded a most vnpleasing harmony.[80]

[sig. E3^v]

He that will be diligent to know, and carefull to obserue the true allowances, may be bolde in his composition, and shall proue quickly ready in his sight, doing that safely and resolutely which others attempt tymerously and vncertainely. But now let vs proceede in the passages of the lesser third.

Thirdly, the lesser third passeth into an eight, the [sig. E4ʳ] lower part descending by degrees, and the vpper part by leaps; but very seldome when the vpper part riseth by degrees, and the lower part falls by a leap.

Fourthly, the lesser third passeth into other Concords, as when it is continued as in degrees[81] it may be, but not in leaps. Also it may passe into the greater third, both by degrees and leaps, as also into the lesser sixt if one of the parts stand still. Into the great[er] sixt it sometime passeth, but very rarely.

Lastly, adde vnto the rest this passage of the lesser third into the lesser sixt, as when the lower part riseth by degrees, and the vpper part by leaps.

[sig. E4ᵛ]

Of the greater or perfect Third.

The greater or perfect third being to passe into perfect Concords, first takes the vnison, when the parts ascend together, the higher by degree, the lower by leap; or when they meete together in a contrary motion, or when one of the parts stand still. Secondly it passeth into a fift when one of the parts rests, as hath beene declared before: or else when the parts ascend or descend together one by degrees, the other by leaps; and so the greater tenth may passe into a fift; seldome when both parts leape together, or when they seperate themselues by degrees; and this is in regard of the relation not harmonicall[82] which falls in betweene the parts. Thirdly, the greater third passeth into the eight by contrary motions, the vpper part ascending by degree.

[sig. E5ʳ] The greater third may also passe into other Concords; and first into a lesser third, when the parts ascend or descend by degrees, or by the lesser leaps. Secondly it is continued, but rarely because it falls into Relation not harmonicall, thereby making the harmony lesse pleasing. Thirdly, into a lesser sixt, when the parts part asunder, the one by degree, the other by leap. Fourthly, into a greater sixt one of the parts standing, or else the vpper part falling by degree, and the lower by leap.

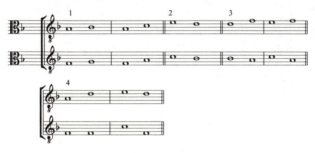

Of the lesser Sixt.

The lesser sixt regularly goes into the fift, one of the parts holding his place: Rarely into an eight, and first when the parts ascend or descend together, and one of them proceeds by the halfe Note, the other by leap.[83]

[sig. E5ᵛ]

Howsoeuer the waies of rising and falling from the lesser sixt into the eight, in the former example may passe, I am sure that if the Base be sharpe in *Ffavt,* it is not tollerable to rise from a sixt to an eight.

Lastly, the lesser sixt may passe into an eight in Crotchets, for they are easily tollerated.

It passeth likewise into other Concords, as into a greater sixt the parts rising or falling by degrees, as [sig. E6ʳ] also into a greater or lesser third, the one part proceeding by degree, the other by leap; or when one of the parts stands. It selfe it cannot follow, by reason of the falling in of the Relation not harmonicall.

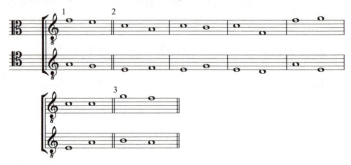

Of the greater Sixt.

The greater sixt in proceeding affects[84] the eight; but it will hardly passe into the fift, vnlesse it be in binding wise,[85] or when way is prepared for a close.

Finally, the greater sixt may in degrees be continued, or passe into a lesser sixt, as also into a greater third, or a lesser third.

[sig. E6ᵛ]

These are the principall obseruations belonging to the passages of Concords, perfect and imperfect, in few parts; and yet in those few for fuge and formality sake,[86] some dispensation may be graunted. But in many parts necessity enforcing, if any thing be committed contrary to rule, it may the more easily be excused, because the multitude of parts will drowne any small inconuenience.[87]

FINIS.

Notes

[1]   On the significance of the dedication see Introduction, pp. 5–7.
[2]   For a discussion of Apollo, David, and the musician-kings and their symbolism see R. Headlam Wells, *Elizabethan Mythologies* (Cambridge: Cambridge University Press, 1994), 63–80. For a common Elizabethan topical allusion to the symbolic persona of Apollo see Campion's ayre 'To his sweet Lute *Apollo* sung the motions of the Spheares' (*Fourth Booke*, viii).
[3]   Campion received his MD at Caen University in 1605. See further I. A. Shapiro, 'Thomas Campion's Medical Degree', *Notes & Queries*, 117 (1957), 495. Campion first styled himself 'Doctor of Phisicke' on the title page of his *The Discription of a Maske* presented in honour of the Lord Hayes, published in 1607.
[4]   Claudius Galenus, *De pulsuum usu* (1522). Galen was well known in England during the sixteenth and seventeenth centuries in various Latin translations, beginning with Linacre (1522): 1529, 1549, 1556, 1562, 1565, 1586. See also M. T. May, *Galen on the Usefulness of the Parts of the Body* (London, 1968).
[5]   The scale was customarily taught, both in England and on the Continent, according to the system of the Gamut (see Introduction, pp. 16–19). Morley begins his *Introduction* (1597) in this fashion. Hortensio's music lesson in Shakespeare's *The Taming of the Shrew* (*c.*1592) commences with the Gamut:

> I must begin with rudiments of art,
> To teach you gamut in a briefer sort (*Shrew* III. i. 64–5)

On concepts associated with 'naming' in the English theoretical system, see further Owens, 'Concepts of Pitch'.
[6]   Ut re mi fa sol la. Campion refers to the restricted vocal range of medieval music which had been expanded in Renaissance music by extending the bass and treble compass.
[7]   On Campion's theory of the scale, see Introduction, pp. 16–21.
[8]   *Works*, ed. Davis, 325, erroneously omits the sixth line of the lute staff.
[9]   Ibid., 326, erroneously omits the sixth line of the lute staff.
[10]   Ibid., 326, erroneously omits the sixth line of the lute staff.

[11] 'Chord' (*Cord*) here and throughout the treatise means a (vertical) interval between consecutive notes and not, as it does today, a triad or vertical assembly of notes sounded simultaneously.

[12] Notable examples include forty-part motets by Alessandro Striggio (*c.*1540–92), *Ecce beatam lucem* (?1568; MS dated 1587) and Thomas Tallis (*c.*1505–85), *Spem in alium* (?1575). Campion may also be referring to multi-choir madrigals by Italian composers such as Giovanni Gabrieli (1557–*c.*1612) and Claudio Monteverdi (1567–1643).

[13] See Introduction, pp. 21–2.

[14] The Four Elements feature symbolically in Campion's *Somerset Masque* (1614). See Wilson, *Campion*, 335. See also Introduction, p. 7. Headlam Wells points out in *Elizabethan Mythologies*, 121, that the strings of the ancient Arabian ʿud, the direct precursor of the Renaissance lute, were symbolically identified with the four elements and were described 'in terms that anticipate Wither's seventeenth-century cosmic lute:

The treble string is like the element of fire, its tone being hot and violent.

The second string is like the element of air; its tone corresponds to the humidity of air and to its softness.

The third string is like the element of water; its tone suggests water-like moisture and coolness.

The bass string is like the heaviness and thickness of the element earth.' (p. 121) (From Eric Werner and Isaiah Sonne, 'The Philosophy and Theory of Music in Judaeo-Arabic Literature', *Hebrew Union College Annual*, 16 (1941), 276.)

[15] At this point, Christopher Simpson adds an explanatory annotation to his later reprint of Campion's text in John Playford's *A Brief Introduction to the Skill of Musick*, published in 1660: 'Counterpoint, in Latin *Contra punctum*, was the old manner of Composing parts together, by setting Points or Pricks one against another (as Minums and Semibriefs are set in this following Treatise,) the measure of which Points or Pricks, were sung according to the quantity of the Words or Syllables to which they were applyed. (For these Figures ᗚ ☐ ◇ were not as yet invented.) And, because in Plain-song Musick we set Note against Note, as they did point against point, thence it is that this kind of Musick doth still retain the name of *Counterpoint*.' (Playford, 94)

[16] This is an early use of the term in a purely musical sense to mean a principal melody part. Morley's use (*Introduction*, 165) is more complicated and rhetorical: 'your plainsong is as it were your theme, and your descant … as it were your declamation'. Zarlino identifies the tenor (plainsong) as a 'theme': 'select a theme or passage and begin to write counterpoints upon this subject' (*Istitutioni*, iii, trans. Marco and Palisca, 154).

[17] Strictly speaking, the 'melody'. This would be more appropriate to the treble, but Campion wishes to emphasise that the bass and not the tenor has the 'theme'. Or he may simply intend that the bass contains within its contour the 'germ' of what the top part may or may not become, in that the treble's shape and movement will be defined by reference to the bass. The second part of the clause (on key) seems to reinforce this idea.

[18] i.e., 'Rules'. It is doubtful if Campion intends a pun although a bass theme could be a 'ground' and he advocates working counterpoint from the bass.

[19] Morley defines 'formality' as 'to make your descant carry some form of relation to the plainsong' (*Introduction*, 149). Whilst Campion does not imply this relationship he does signify a 'strict' rather than a 'free' bass observing rules of counterpoint.

[20] A term used elsewhere by Campion in a musical context, e.g., 'Author of number, that hath all the world in / Harmonie framed' from 'Come, let us sound' (*A Booke of Ayres*, 1601, xxi).

[21] i.e., by step or conjunct movement. Campion employs this term, 'by degrees', frequently in the treatise.

[22] Simpson annotation: 'If the Bass do rise more then a fourth, it must be called falling: and likewise, if it fall any distance more then a fourth, that falling must be called rising.' (Playford, 96)

[23] Simpson annotation: 'If your Bass should fall a seventh, it is the same as if it did rise a second, or a sixth falling is but the same of a third rising: and so on the contrary, if the Bass do rise a seventh or sixth, it is the same as though it did fall a second or a third.' (Playford, 96)

[24] A perhaps not unintentional gibe at Morley's *A Plaine and Easie Introduction to Practicall Musicke* (1597).

[25] Campion's 'infallible' rule shown in his little table of six figures between consecutive chords in four voices, each chord containing a third, fifth and octave, or their compounds, above the bass. Thus, if the bass rises a second, third or fourth, the part which is a third above the bass falls to the octave; the fifth goes to a third and the octave proceeds to the fifth. In other words, read the table upwards. If the bass descends a second, third or fourth then the table should be read downwards so that the octave falls to the third; the third descends to the fifth and the fifth goes to the octave. The table also works in a passage where the bass both rises and falls.

[26] Simpson annotation: 'By their Compounds is meant their Octaves, as a third and its eights, a fifth and its eights, &c.' (Playford, 97)

[27] Simpson annotation: 'Example of all the three parts added to the Bass.' (Playford, 98)

[28] Simpson annotation: 'When you have made a formal Bass, and would joyn other three parts to it, set the first Note of your Tenor either a third, fifth, or eighth above your Bass, (which of them you please) which done, place your Mean in the next Cord you find above your Tenor, and your Treble in the next Cord above your Mean, then follow the Rule of your figures, according to the rising or falling of your Bass, and the other Notes will follow in their due order.' (Playford, 102)

[29] Simpson annotation: 'If this Discourse of Cords under the Bass do trouble the young beginner, let him think no more upon them (for it is not intended that he should place any Notes below the Bass) but let him look for his Cords, reckoning always from his Bass upward; which that he may more easily perform, let him draw eleven lines (which is the whole compass of the Scale) and set the three used Cliffs in their proper places; this done, he may prick his Bass in the lowest five lines, and then set the other three parts in their orderly distances above the Bass, Note against Note, as you see in this Example. [Example of 11-line staff; see Introduction, p. 13] which being prick'd in several parts, appeareth thus: [Example of Treble, Mean, Tenor, Bass]' (Playford, 103–4).

I have proposed the former Example of the eleven lines, to lead the young beginner to a true knowledge of the Scale, without which nothing can be effected; but having once got that knowledge, let him then Compose his Musick in several parts, as he seeth in his second Example.

Here I think it not amiss to advertise the young Beginner, that so often as the Bass doth fall a fifth, or rise a fourth (which is all one, as hath been said) that part which is a third to the Bass in the antecedent Note, that third I say must always be the sharp or greater third, as was apparent in the last example of four parts, in the first Notes of the second Bar in the Mean Part, and likewise in the last Note but one of the same part, in both which places there is a ✳ set to make it the greater third. The same is to be observ'd in what part soever this third shall happen.' (Playford, 104–5)

[30] i.e., according to the rules of counterpoint.

[31] 'Breaking' is a technical term to mean dividing longer notes into shorter notes without affecting the harmony, so here a semibreve becomes four crotchets. Usually the

shorter notes, the 'divisions', proceed rising or falling in conjunct movement. There is a large sixteenth- and early seventeenth-century literature on 'divisions'; see H. M. Brown, *Embellishing Sixteenth-Century Music* (Oxford, 1976); V. Duckles, 'Florid Embellishment in English Song of the Late 16th and Early 17th Centuries', *Annales musicologiques*, 5 (1957), 329–45; R. Toft, *Tune thy Musicke to thy Hart: The Art of Eloquent Singing in England, 1597–1622* (Toronto, 1993), 85–99.

[32]   'censure': *obs.* meaning 'work out', 'estimate', 'deduce' in this context.

[33]   Simpson annotation: 'When your Bass standeth still (that is to say, hath two or more Notes together in one and the same place) you may chuse whether you will make your parts do so too, or change them, as you see our Author hath done in the Second Note of this present example. If you change them, you may do it either by the Rule of descending or ascending, which you please, so you do but observe formality.' (Playford, 107 [printed 207])

[34]   If the bass implies a first-inversion chord then substitute a 6 for the 5 in the lower line of the table, thus

8	3	5
3	6	8

and observe the rule as before.

[35]   *Works*, ed. Davis, 335: Davis's tenor should be read in the bass (F) clef and not in the treble (G) clef.

[36]   If the bass contains F♯ or E♭ then care must be taken not to double the bass note, the exception to his rule, the E♭ proceeding to D major would result in an augmented second, which is 'unformall'.

[37]   On this remarkable passage, see Introduction, pp. 24–6. Simpson annotation: 'He doth not mean, that such Basses are bad, false, or defective, but that they have (perhaps for elegancy or variety) assumed the nature of some part for a Note or two, and so want the full latitude of a Bass in those Notes.' (Playford, 109)

[38]   See Introduction, pp. 24–6.

[39]   In the original, the tenor (third note) has a printed C altered to a B♭. The B♭ is correct. *Works*, ed. Davis, 336, keeps the C, thereby creating parallel fifths with the treble. Davis also changes the rhythm of the first bar of the meane.

[40]   A reference to the conventional Renaissance final cadential *tierce* in a minor key.

[41]   Original has 'unformall', referring to the concept of the 'formal' bass (see p. 46 and above, n. 19).

[42]   i.e., same meaning as above (see n. 31). Here the 'division' in the bass is descending.

[43]   Simpson annotation: 'When any informality doth occur, the Scholar need not tye himself to the first Rules of the Bass rising or falling, but may take such Cords at [*sic*] his Genius shall prompt him to, (having a care that he take not two eights or fifts together, rising or falling betwixt any two parts whatsoever: 'Tis true, our Author did invent this Rule of the figures, as the easiest way to lead the young Beginner to this kind of Composition, in which he hath done more then any that I have ever seen upon this subject; but this he did to show the smoothest way, and not to tye his Scholar to keep strictly that way when a block or stone should happen to lye in it, but that he may in such a case step out of this way for a Note or two, and then return again into it.' (Playford, 113)

[44]   Campion objects to two consecutive first inversions if the 'sixes' are in the treble. His reason(s) are not clear except that if two first inversions are written his 'infallible' rule is broken because a third is followed by a third, and a sixth by a sixth. Campion's explanation, which follows, is illogical in the modern, tonal harmonic sense. Consecutive fourths in the inner voices are perfectly acceptable.

[45]   i.e., resolved into an octave or unison.

[46] i.e., bar or measure.

[47] *Works*, ed. Davis, 341, misaligns the treble and bass in all the examples. On the relationship of this passage to Coprario's *Rules*, see Introduction, pp. 7–10.

[48] Simpson annotation: 'Counterpoint is the first part and ground of Composition; the second part of it is figurative Musick or Descant, which mixeth fast and slow Notes together, bindeth Discords with Concords and maketh one part to answer another in point or Fuge, with many other excellent varieties: to the attaining of which I cannot commend you to a better Authour, than our most excellent Country-man, Mr. *Morley*, in the second and third part of his Introduction to Musick. If you desire to see what Forain Authours do write on this subject, you may (if you understand Latine) peruse the works of *Athenasius Kirkerus* and *Marsenus*, two excellent late Authours,

But first peruse the two little Treatises following in this present Book; the one of the Tones of Musick; the other of passages of Concords; in both which our Authour (according to his accustomed Method) doth more briefly and more perspicuously treat, then any other Author you shall meet with on the same subject.' (Playford, 118)

[49] I have been unable to find another source for this 'short hymn'. Its text is a conflated metrical paraphrase of phrases from certain verses of several different psalms. Three of the Penitential Psalms include those phrases, but no single one of them is exactly parallel to Campion's words.

Ps. 6 has:

> v. ii '*Have mercy upon me, O Lord*; for I am weak: O Lord, heal me; for my bones are vexed.'

> v. vi 'I am weary with my groaning; *all the night* make I my bed to swim; *I water my couch with tears.*'

Ps. 42 has:

> v. iii '*My tears* have been my meat *day and night* …

> v. iv 'When I remember these things, *I pour out my soul* in me …

Ps. 39 has:

> v. xii '*Hear my prayer, O Lord*, and give ear unto my cry; hold not thy peace *at my tears.*'

Other psalms which include Campion's words are Pss. 22 vv. 1–2, 42 v. 10, 55 v. 18. *Works*, ed. Davis, 342, has a final C in the bass. The G in the original is correct.

[50] A reference to the English preference for 'sweet' thirds and sixths, originating in the fifteenth century. The final chord includes a major third (B♮) in the tenor which according to the rules should have been an open fifth (D). Campion says the full triad with the third is preferred because it sounds 'sweeter', and because slight deviation from the rules governing the progression of parts is not so obvious in an 'inner' part. The presence of the major third relates to his earlier point (see n. 40) about a final *tierce* in a minor key.

[51] Campion conflates these terms. In Renaissance theory and practice, key, tone and mode are not the same. A mode with no signature and a *finalis* on D, for example, is not the same as a key of D with one (or two) sharps. A (Psalm) tone is not equivalent to a mode. Campion seems to derive the sense of this first paragraph from Morley:

> every key hath a peculiar air proper unto itself, so that if you go into another than that wherein you begun you change the air of the song, which is as much as to wrest a thing out of his nature, making the ass leap upon his master and the spaniel bear the load. The perfect knowledge of these airs (which the antiquity termed 'Modi') was in such estimation amongst the learned as therein they placed the perfection of music, as you may perceive at large in the fourth book of Severinus Boethius his *Music*; and Glareanus hath written a learned book which he took in hand only for the explanation of these modes; and though the air of every key be different one from the other yet some love (by a wonder of nature) to be joined to others, so that if you begin your song in Gam ut you may conclude it either in C fa ut or D sol re and from thence

come again to Gam ut; likewise if you begin your song in D sol re you may end in A re and come again to D sol re, etc.

PHIL.   Have you no general rule to be given for an instruction for keeping of the key?

MA.   No, for it must proceed only of the judgement of the composer; yet churchmen for keeping their keys have devised certain notes commonly called the Eight Tunes [i.e., Psalm tones], so that according to the tune which is to be observed at that time, if it begin in such a key it may end in such and such others, as you shall immediately know. And these be, although not the true substance, yet some shadow of the ancient 'modi' whereof Boethius and Glareanus have written so much. (*Introduction*, 249)

On this passage by Morley see Owens, 'Concepts of Pitch', 218–20. In confusing (Psalm) tone with mode, Morley betrays his unfamiliarity with Continental practices. Similarly, Campion reveals his misunderstanding of Continental systems and his dependence on Morley in claiming 'Key' to be a compound of named pitches, properties ('correct' and strange), and individual mood or character ('aire'). See also Owens, 'Concepts of Pitch', 220–24.

[52] Frans Wiering, *The Language of the Modes: Studies in the History of Polyphonic Modality* (New York and London: Routledge, 2001), 215, says that Campion 'describes Zarlino's double division of the octave, probably after Calvisius 1600' (i.e., *Exercitationes musicae duae*).

[53] i.e., 'Authentic' mode. The genus is determined by the *finalis* and the position of the 'dominant' or fifth. On modes see further H. Powers and F. Wiering, 'Mode', §III, in *The New Grove Dictionary of Music and Musicians*, 2nd edn, ed. S. Sadie and J. Tyrrell (London: Macmillan, 2001). See also Lester, 'Major-Minor Concepts', 209–17. Campion employs these modal terms loosely. In fact, his definition is more applicable to his concept of 'key' than to aspects of 'neo-modal' theory.

[54] i.e., 'Plagal' mode. Again identified by the *finalis* and 'dominant', used loosely in the context of 'key' rather than mode.

[55] See Introduction, pp. 23–4.

[56] In other words, determining whether the key is major or minor. In polyphonic music of the Renaissance, the place of the mediant had begun to play an important role in determining the mode, especially the authentic mode. It was less predictable in the plagal modes.

[57] See Introduction, pp. 23–4. *Works*, ed. Davis, 344, misaligns the treble and bass.

[58] See Introduction, pp. 23–4. The melody and bass he quotes is his 'Fire that must flame', *Third Booke*, xv. From bar 8, regular bar lines have been inserted for the sake of clarity. In bar 6, the bass (second note) is an A, not B as found in the original. The ayre has the A. *Works*, ed. Davis, 345, reproduces the error. Campion gives the melody and bass of this short ayre in their entirety, unlike the other ayres he quotes.

In fact, this example, lacking B♭s, is rather modal than tonal. It is, therefore, not as valid as if there had been a B♭, making the A minor cadence a dominant of the relative minor (D minor). But this is how it is printed both in the *Third Booke of Ayres* and in the treatise. Playford/Simpson, however, were clearly aware of the problem and introduce a B♭ into the key signature (1660 edn, p. 223 [*recte* p. 123]), thus significantly affecting bar 2.

[59] See Introduction, p. 24.

[60] Bar 3: B♮. Original has B♭, reproduced in *Works*, ed. Davis, 345.

[61] They are respectively, 'Turne all thy thoughts', *Fourth Booke*, xx, and 'Young and simple though I am', *Fourth Booke*, ix. There are minor rhythmical differences between

the ayres and the examples. In the first, bar 3 of the ayre (bass) has ♩♩, and bar 4 (treble) ♩♪♩; in the second, bars 2 and 4 (bass) have ♩♩.

[62] Thomas East (ed.), *The Whole Booke of Psalms: With Their Wonted Tunes, as they are sung in Churches, composed into four parts ..Compiled by Sondry Authors* (1592).

[63] Thomas East referred to this tune as one used 'in most churches of this realme' for chanting psalms. It was first published in the 1564 Scottish psalter set to Ps. 108. It subsequently appeared in almost every English and Scottish psalter up to the early eighteenth century, known variously as either 'Oxford' or 'Old Common' (see further, Introduction, pp. 11–12 and n. 28). In the music example, note 11 (F) is properly a crotchet. *Works*, ed. Davis, 347, has a minim. Note 14 (B) has to be altered to a B♭ according to the rules of *musica ficta*, and to agree with what must be a B♭ in Campion's composed bass. *Works*, ed. Davis, 347, has B♮. On *musica ficta* see further Nicholas Routley, 'A Practical Guide to Musica Ficta', *Early Music*, 13 (1985), 59–71, and Karol Berger, *Musica Ficta: Theories of Accidental Inflections in Vocal Polyphony from Marchetto da Padova to Gioseffo Zarlino* (Cambridge, 1987).

[64] The original has an E♭ key signature. It should include a B♭ (which is missing). *Works*, ed. Davis, 347, reproduces E♭ only.

[65] A 'shift' is an expedient or way of contriving a means to an end. Morley (*Introduction,* 174) employs the word with this meaning:

MA.   .But why did you stand so long before the close?

PHIL.   Because I saw none other way to come to it.

MA.   Yet there is shift enough; but why did you stand still with your last note also seeing there was no necessity in that?

Campion says that the original tune begins in F (major) and ends in G minor. The alteration or 'shift' is remarkable in the context of the psalm tune and is not clearly explained. Owens ('Concepts of Pitch', 222), says, 'I am not certain how to interpret [Campion's] remarks: does he mean the contrasting kinds of thirds in the melodic contour F–G–A as opposed to [F]–G–A–B♭ or the different sounds of the F "major" opening sonority compared to the G "minor" final sonority?' See the Introduction, pp. 11–12, for the harmonisations by Kirbye and Ravenscroft and further discussion.

[66] The tune is in the tenor, which is altered to fit the key of G minor.

[67] i.e., the chord of the dominant.

[68] cf. Campion's 'Come, let us sound' (*A Booke of Ayres*, 1601, xxi): 'Author of number, that hath all the world in / Harmonie framed' (lines 3–4).

[69] See Introduction, p. 29.

[70] See Introduction, pp. 30–33.

[71] Consecutive octaves and fifths in counterpoint are forbidden.

[72] Campion makes this point several times in his treatise, that in polyphony of many voices (commonly five or more) various less good progressions are permissible. This is certainly true, for example, in the works of Palestrina and Lassus, representatives of the highest art of Renaissance counterpoint. On this, see, for example, H. K. Andrews, *An Introduction to the Technique of Palestrina* (London, 1958), 63–8, where he discusses so-called prohibited consecutive fifths and octaves (by contrary motion) and consecutive major thirds.

[73] 'The same is true of octaves.' This point is found in Calvisius, ΜΕΛΟΠΟΙΙΑ, sig. C2ᵛ. See Introduction, p. 30.

[74] *Works*, ed. Davis, 350, gives these examples in reverse order to the original.

[75] False or cross-relation. See Introduction, pp. 32–3.

[76] Campion is here referring to the false or cross-relation occurring in four-part polyphony. Its presence would indeed create 'strange discord' to tonal ears.

[77] 'only saying', i.e., truism. 'Only' is used here in *obs.* form meaning esteemed, unique in quality (*OED*).

[78] 'Mi and Fa are [the substance] of all music.' Compare Campion's 'The Preface', above, p. 43.

[79]   unmusical/immusicall.

[80]   He quotes the opening strains of his 'A Secret love or two I must confess', *Two Bookes II*, xix. Extra accidentals are required, which are confirmed in the ayre, to avoid 'imperfect' or augmented seconds in the treble: bar 2 E♮, bar 7 E♮, bar 9 E♮, bar 13 E♮. *Works*, ed. Davis, 352, has E♭s throughout. Otherwise, this example and the ayre agree. Campion omits the last three strains of the ayre in his example.

[81]   i.e., by step or conjunct movement.

[82]   'False relation'. Compare n. 75.

[83]   The final note of the lower (tenor) voice should be A. The original has B♭, reproduced in *Works*, ed. Davis, 354.

[84]   'Desires' [to move to] the octave.

[85]   Tied over or suspended, as in bars 2–4 of the example.

[86]   In strict rules of imitative counterpoint.

[87]   Compare n. 72.

Giovanni Coprario
Rules how to Compose

Introduction and Editorial Note

Although Coprario's manuscript, entitled *Rules how to Compose*, has been available in a well-presented facsimile edition since 1952,[1] this is the first time that it has been edited and published in its original form in a modern volume. The reader wishing to know more about the context and content of Coprario's treatise should consult the introduction to that edition. Bukofzer (p. 2) includes a brief description of the manuscript treatise as follows:

> The manuscript consists of forty unnumbered folios written by one hand … The original binding in limp vellum is inscribed "Gio: Coprario" and "J. Bridgewater" in the hand of the owner. Originally, the title page read only "Rules how to Compose." The name of the author was subsequently supplied at the top of the page by J. Egerton who entered his own name under the title. After he had been made Earl of Bridgewater (in 1617) he signed the book once more by his new name in justifiable pride. This accounts for the signature "J. Bridgewater" written in bolder letters but with fewer flourishes. The double signature proves that the manuscript must have been in Egerton's possession before 1617 and thus gives the latest possible date for the compilation of the treatise. The watermarks of the paper can be dated between 1594 and 1614. On the basis of this evidence the manuscript has been assigned the date of c. 1610.

Although there are several autograph manuscripts purporting to be in the hand of Coprario, it now seems as though the *Rules how to Compose* is the authenticated copy. The evidence for this comes from Richard Charteris, whose research has uncovered a letter at Hatfield House in North London bearing an autograph matching that found in the Huntington manuscript.[2]

An as yet unsolved question concerning the *Rules how to Compose* is the method by which Coprario's treatise came to be so well known. Since there is only one extant manuscript, no printed editions or earlier facsimiles, how were its contents so widespread? Moreover, the condition of the autograph manuscript is so good that it does not seem likely that it has been heavily consulted. The manuscript itself has a clear and brief provenance. It came into the possession of the Huntington Library in 1917 when it was purchased by Mr Huntington as part of the Bridgewater Library of manuscripts and printed books. This library belonged to the Egerton family – the Earls and Dukes of Bridgewater and the Earls of Ellesmere. It is likely that the manuscript had been in this library from the time it was written. It may even have been a presentation copy, although there is no dedicatory letter. Both the 1st Earl and his father Lord Chancellor Ellesmere were keen literary collectors and it is conceivable that they may have allowed consultation of the manuscript, even without publication.[3] Another possibility might be that its influence stems from connections with Campion's treatise *A New Way of Making Fowre Parts in Counterpoint*; that it is through Campion's book that Coprario's ideas were brought forth. At present, however, this can be no more than speculation.

The text of the manuscript is presented here as it appears in the original except where the scribe has made corrections to obvious mistakes, in which case the amended version is given.

The use of capitalised and small (minuscule) characters has also been preserved – in particular, the use of a small 'i' at the start of sentences or phrases beginning 'if …'. The decision to preserve this form has been made because it seems as though Coprario's intention was to present a list of criteria which the composer (of counterpoint) should follow. In view of this, Coprario's prose at these points may be seen as a continuous run-on of ideas relating to one larger point. The fact that each new line starts with 'if' does not necessarily imply a different sentence, merely a list of consequent points to consider.

Similarly, the orthography of the manuscript has neither been modernised nor regularised, and variations, where they occur, have been preserved. In order to aid the modern reader, obscure, significantly varied or obsolete words and meanings are explained in the notes.

Notes

[1]　Giovanni Coperario, *Rules how to Compose*, facs. edn with an introduction by Manfred Bukofzer (Los Angeles: Ernest E. Gottlieb, 1952).
[2]　Richard Charteris, 'Autographs of John Coprario', *Music & Letters*, 56 (1975), 41–6.
[3]　I am grateful to Mary Robertson, Curator of Manuscripts at the Huntington Library, for these details.

Giovanni Coprario.
Rules
how to Compose

Rules how to Compose

Concords from the Bass uppward

Ffaut	the	3	Alamire
		5	Csolfaut
		6	Dlasolre[.]

Elami	the	3	Gsolreut
		5	Bfabmi
		6	Csolfaut.

Dlasolre	the	3	ffaut
		5	Alamire
		6	Bfabmi.

Csolfaut	the	3	Elami
		5	Gsolreut
		6	Alamire.

Bfabmi	the	3	Dlasolre
		5	ffaut
		6	Gsolreut.

Alamire	the	3	Csolfaut
		5	Elami
		6	ffaut.

Gamut, or Gsolreut	the	3	Bfabmi
		5	Dlasolre
		6	Elami.

Concords from the Canto downeward

Ffaut	the	3	Dlasolre
		5	Bfabmi
		6	Alamire.

Elami	the	3	Csolfaut
		5	Alamire
		6	Gsolreut[.]

Dlasolre   the   3   Bfabmi
                     5   Gsolreut
                     6   ffaut[.]

Csolfaut   the   3   Alamire
                     5   ffaut
                     6   Elami.

Bfabmi   the   3   Gsolreut
                     5   Elami
                     6   Dlasolre[.]

Alamire   the   3   ffaut
                     5   Dlasolre
                     6   Csolfaut.

Gsolreut   the   3   Elami
                     5   Csolfaut
                     6   Bfabmi.

A vnison is good so it be in a minim, or a chrochett, butt a vnison is better so the one hold, and the other be going from thence.

[fol. 2ᵛ]

Perfect chords
the

	3:	5:	6:	8:
octaves.	10:17:	12:19:	13:20:	15:22:

Imperfect chords
the

	2:	4:	7:	9:
octaves.		11:18:	14:21:	16:23:

Two eights, and two fifts, ore their octaves
are unlawfull.

What chords parts are to vse.
if Canto vse the 8, Alto vses the 5, Tenor the 3.
if Canto vse the 12, Alto vses the 10, Tenor the 8.
if Canto vse the 10, Alto vses the 8, Tenor the 5.
if Canto vse the 5, Alto vses the 3, Tenor must vse the vnison with the Bass, or elss Alto maie vse the Vnison with Canto, and then Tenor must vse the 3.

[fol. 3ʳ]

How to com, from a Discord

if you vse a 4, or 11, your next note must be a 3, or 10.

if you vse a 9, your next note must be the 8.

if you vse a 7, your next note must be the 6.

if you vse a 2, your next note must be the 3.

if you vse a false fift, your next note must be the 3.

if Basso vse a sharpe the 8 is nott to be taken in Diatonic songs, butt the 8 underneath the 10, or elss the vnison of the 3, Neither is the 5 to be vsd, butt the 6 in steed of the 5.

if the song be flatt in Bfabmi ascend with Elami sharpe, and descend with Elami flatt, except it be a 5, or 12.

if Basso rise a 2, 4, or fall a 5, or a sharpe 3 then the 10, or 3 if it ascend should be made sharpe.

No part ought to descend with ffaut, Csolfaut, or Gsolreut sharpe, neither ought you to descend with Bfabmi sharpe, if the song be flatt in Bfabmi, except chromatic songs in the which of necessitie you shall be forced, by the reason they will descend sharpe, and vse either 5, or 8. Butt in songs Diatonic you must shunn to descend with sharps in ffavt, Csolfavt, Gsolreut, and Bfabmi sharpe so the song be flatt in Bfabmi.

[fol. 3ᵛ]

Rules of rising, and falling one with another

it is not good to rise with the Bass from a 12 vnto an 8, or from an 8 vnto a 5. Neither is it good to fall with the Bass from an 8 vnto a 12, or from a 5 vnto an 8 as for example.

you ought to shunn for to rise with the Bass from a 6, vnto an 8, likewise you maie doe well in shunning to fall with the Bass from an 8 vnto a 6.

as for example.

[fol. 4^r]

if Basso meanes to make a close.

The Bass meanes to make a close when he rises a 5, 2, or 3, and then falls a 5, or rises a 4. Likewise if the Bass fall a 4, or 2, and then fall a 5, he meanes to vse a close, then that part must hold, which in holding can vse the 11, or 4 with the Bass in the next note rising, or falling, and then you must vse either the 3, or 10.

as for example

here the 10 is vsd

Here the 3 is vsd.

The holding consists in the 4, or 11

[fol. 4^v]

What chords parts are to vse in Contrapoinct.

if the Bass rise a 2, Canto demaunds a 10, next an 8, Alto first an 8, next a 5, Tenor first an 8, next a 3.

if Canto vse two 10 together, Alto vses an 8, next a 5, Tenor vses a 5, next a 3.

if Canto vse a 12, and next a 10, Alto must vse the 10, and then an 8, Tenor must vse the 8, next the 5.

if Canto vse the 15, and next the 12, Alto must vse the 12, next the 10, Tenor must vse the 10, next the 8.

as for example

[fol. 5ʳ]

if the Bass fall a 2 Canto maie first vse the 8, next the 10, Alto the 5, next the 8, Tenor the 3, next the 5.

if Canto first vse the 10, and next the 12, Alto demaunds first the 8, next the 10, Tenor the 5, next the 8.

if Canto vse two 10 together, Alto first demaunds the 5, next the 8, Tenor the 3, or 8, next the 5.

if Canto first vse the 12, next the 15, Alto vses first the 10, next the 12, Tenor vses the 8, next the 10.

[fol. 5ᵛ]

if the Bass fall a 3, Canto first maie vse an 8, next a 10, Alto maie vse the 5, next the 8, Tenor vses the 3, next the 5.

if Canto vse first the 10, next the 12, Alto vses the 8, next the 10, Tenor the 5, next the 8.

if Canto vse two 10 together, Alto first vses the 5, next the 8, Tenor the 3, next the 5.

if Canto first vse the 12, next the 15, Alto first vses the 10, next the 12, Tenor the 8, next the 10.

[fol. 6ʳ]

if the Bass rise a 3 Canto maie first vse the 10, next the 8, Alto first the 8, next the 5, Tenor first the 5, next the 3.

if Canto first vse the 12, next the 10, Alto first vses the 10, next the 8, Tenor the 8, next the 5.

if Canto vse two 10 together, Alto first vses the 8, next the 5, Tenor vses the 5, next the 3.

if Canto vse first the 15, next the 12, Alto vses the 12, next the 10, Tenor vses first the 10, next the 8.

[fol. 6ᵛ]

if the Bass fall a 4 Canto first maie vse an 8, next the 10, Alto the 5, next the 8, Tenor the 3, next the 5:

if Canto first vse the 10, next the 12, Alto must vse the 8, next the 10, Tenor the 5, next the 8.

if Canto first vse the 5, next the 10, Alto must vse the 3, next the 8, Tenor must first vse the Vnison with the Bass, next the 5.

if Canto vse first the 12, next the 15, Alto vses the 10, next the 12, Tenor vses the 8, next the 10.

[fol. 7ʳ]

if the Bass rise a 4 Canto first maie vse the 10, next the 8, Alto the 8, next the 5, Tenor the 5, next the 3.

if Canto first vse the 12, next the 10, Alto vses the 10, next the 8, Tenor the 8, next the 5.

if Canto first vse the 15, next the 12, Alto vses the 12, next the 10, Tenor the 10, next the 8.

if Canto first vse the 10, next the 12, Alto vses the 12, next the 10, Tenor the 8, next the 5[.]

[fol. 7ᵛ]
if the Bass fall a 5, you maie vse thesam chords, the which you vse when the
Bass rises a 4.

[fol. 8ʳ]
if the Bass rise a 5, you maie vse thesam chords, the which you vse when the
Bass falls a 4.

[fol. 8ᵛ]
if the Bass fall an 8, you maie lett Canto rise from the 8 vnto the 17, Alto maie
rise from the 5 vnto the 15 so he hold his 5, Tenor maie rise from the 3 vnto the
12. Or elss you maie lett your parts stand still, as lett Canto the 8, next the 15,
Alto the 5, next the 12, Tenor the 3, next the 10.

   The Bass falling it is nott good for the inner parts for to fall with him, butt
when Basso falls a parte maie rise, and it will shew well.

[fol. 9ʳ]

if the Bass rise an 8, Canto first maie vse the 15, and next the 8, or elss holding the 15 next maie vse the 10, Alto first vses the 12, next the 5, Tenor vses the 10, next the 3.

The Bass rising it is nott good for any other parte for to rise with him, butt when Basso rises another parte maie fall, and it will goe well.

[fol. 9ᵛ]

How to vse a 6 in Contrapoinct

A 6 in Contrapoinct is vsed when the Bass falls a 3, or rises a 3, 2, or 4.

if the Bass fall a 3 and then rise a 2, Canto first maie vse a 10, next the 13, Alto the 8, next the 10, Tenor the 5, next the 8.

if Canto first vse the 12, next the 15, Alto must vse the 10, next the 13, Tenor the 8, next the 10.

if Canto vse first the 8, next the 10, Alto must vse the 5, next the 8, Tenor the 3, next the 6.

if Canto vse two 10 together, Alto must vse first the 5, next the 8, Tenor the 3, next the 6.

These rules shewing how to vse a 6 in Contrapoint are onlie to be observed in minims, and chrocchetts, in semibreves you must nott vse thesam.

[fol. 10ʳ]
if the Bass rise a 3 and then fall a 2 Canto first maie vse a 15, next the 10, Alto the 10, next the 8 he must divide, and then vse the 10, Tenor the 8, next the 5.
if Canto vse the 15, next the 12, Alto must vse the 13, next the 10, Tenor the 10, next the 8 he must divide, and then vse the 10.
if Canto vse two 10 together, Alto first maie vse the 8 next the 5, Tenor the 6, next the 3.

The last example is faultie, and the fault is between Canto, and Alto in the 3 note: Alto rises with Canto vsing a false 4, wherefore you must vse [*sic*] divide the second note in Alto, and cause him for to rise vnto the 10, and then com down, and vse the 10, as it appeareth in the first example.

[fol. 10ᵛ]
if the Bass rise seconds[1] for 4 notes together, Canto maie ascend with him vsing all 10, Alto first must vse an 8[,] secondlie a 6, thirdlie a 3, next a 5[,] Tenor first a 5, secondlie an 8, thirdlie a 6, next a 3.
if Canto first vse the 15[,] secondlie the 13, thirdlie the 10, next the 8, Alto must vse 10 for three notes together, and then vse the 5, Tenor must vse the 5 firstlye[,] secondlie the 8, thirdlie the 6, next the 3.

[fol. 11ʳ]
if the Bass rise a 4, or fall a 5 and then fall a 2, next rise a 3, Canto first maie vse the 17, and secondlie, and thirdlie vse two 13 together, and next the 10. Alto

first vses the 12, secondlie the 10 and thirdlie the 10, next the 8, Tenor first vses
the 8, secondlie the 3, thirdlie the 8, and next the 5.
if the Bass fall a 5 the sam is likewise to be observed, as if the Bass should rise a
4.

[fol. 11ᵛ]

of Division.

if anie parte rise a 3 you maie divide the first note into equall notes of proportion, or elss you maie hold the first note with a pricke.

[fol. 12ʳ]

if anie part fall a 3 then you maie divide the first note into equall notes of
proportion, or elss you maie hold the first note with a pricke.

[fol. 12ᵛ]

if anie part rise a 4, you maie divide your first note into three notes, the first note
divided must be halfe, and the other two must be the other halfe, or elss you
maie hold the first with a pricke, and then the rest must be the quarter.

[fol. 13ʳ]

if anie part fall a 4 you maie divide the first note into three notes, and the first
note must be halfe, and the rest must be the other halfe, or elss you maie hold the
first with a pricke, and lett the other two be the quarter.

[fol. 13ᵛ]

if anie part rise a 5, the first note maie be divided into foure notes, or elss you maie hold the first and the third with prickes. butt if they rise in quavers you maie nott vse them with a pricke in a songe.

[fol. 14ʳ]

if any part fall a 5 you maie divide the first note into foure notes, or elss you maie hold them, especiallie the first, and third note with prickes, except it be in quavers.

[fol. 14ᵛ]

if the Bass rise a 3 in devision, Canto maie rise tenths with him[,] Alto first must hold in the 8, next vse the 5[,] Tenor must first hold his 5, and next vse the 3.

[fol. 15ʳ]

if the Bass fall a 3 in devision, Canto maie fall with him in 10, Alto must hold first his 5, next vse the 8, Tenor must hold first the 3, and next vse the 5.

[fol. 15ᵛ]

if the Bass fall a 4 dividing his first note, Canto maie fall with him vsing 10, and
the rest of parts maie hold, or stirre so it be without faults.

[fol. 16ʳ]

if the Bass rise a 4 dividing his first note Canto maie vse tenths, and fall with
him, the rest of parts must hold.

[fol. 16ᵛ]

if the Bass fall a fifte in devision, and com nott vnto a close, you must vse in the
rest of parts to sett vnto the first note of the Bass vntill he com to his fift note,
and if the Bass descend foure chrocchets you maie vse in the rest of parts a
semibreve, if quavers then a minim, or

[fol.17ʳ]

Or elss if the Bass fall a 5 in devision lett the part which vses the 5 vnto the first note vse the 8 vnto the third note of the Bass.

[fol. 17ᵛ]

if the Bass rise a 5 in devision lett Canto vse the 15, and hold and then vse the 10, Alto must vse the 12, and next the 8, Tenor the 10 next the 5.

[fol. 18ʳ]

if the Bass vse semibreves some of the parts maie divide, and goe from the 3 in the 5, or from the 5 into the 8, or from the 8 into the 5, or from the 5 into the 3, or rise from the 8 vnto the 15, and so they maie divide their semibreves either into crochetts, or quavers.

[fol. 18ᵛ]

Of Ligatures
if the Bass rise a 2 how the 10 maie hold.

if the Bass rise 3, or 4 seconds, or after a 2 rise a 3 or fall a 4, or a 3 the part which vses the 10 must hold, and next vse the 8.

This holding is vppon a 9.

The 10 must hold when the Bass ascends 3, or 4 seconds, and then meanes to make a kinde of close vppon the third ascending note.

[fol. 19ʳ]

if the Bass rise a 2 how the 12, or 5 maie hold.

if the Bass rise a seconde and then rise a 4, or fall a 5: or if the Bass rise a 2, and then fall a 4, or 5, or a sharpe 3, lett the part hold which vses the 12, or 5, and then vse the 10.

This holding is vppon the 4, and 11.

The 12, or 5 holds when the Bass rises, and will have his second ascending note to be made a close.

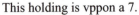

[fol. 19ᵛ]

if the Bass rise a 2 how the 8 or 15 maie hold.

if the Bass rise a 2, and then rise another sharpe 2: or if the Bass rise a 2, and then rise a 3, or fall a 2, lett the part hold which vses the 8, or 15, and then vse a 6, or 13. Or if the Bass rise two 2, and then fall a 5.

This holding is vppon a 7.

[fol. 20ʳ]

if the Bass rise a 2 how the 8 maie hold[.]

if the Bass rise a 2, and then fall a 4 meaning for to change the ayre,[2] and to deferr a close lett the 8 hold, and then vse the 6.

This holding is vppon a 7.

[fol. 20ᵛ]

if the Bass rise a 2 in minims, and then fall a 3 the 8, or 10 maie hold, and vse vnto the third note of the Bass either the 3 or 10.

Here the 8 holds
vsing a 7.

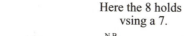

Here the 10 holds
vsing a 9.

[fol. 21^r]

if the Bass ascend three seconds in minims, or chrocchetts the 15, or 8 maie hold, and then vse vnto the third note of the 12 or 5.

The holding is vppon a 7[.]

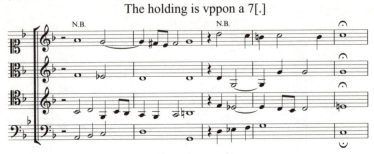

[fol. 21^v]

if the Bass rise two 2 in minims, or chrocchetts, and then fall a 5, you maie vse vnto the second note of the Bass a 6 for a 5.

[fol. 22^r]

if the Bass rise many 2 (seconds),[3] lett the part which vses the 5 divide, and then vse a 6, and so hold as it appeareth in the Tenor in the following example.

[fol. 22ᵛ]

if the Bass rise a 3, and then rise a 2, or fall a 2, a 4, or a 5 lett your part which vses the 12, or 5 divide, and then vse a 6, or 13 holding thesam he must vse the 10, or 3.

This holding is vppon the 11, and 4.

[fol. 23ʳ]

if the Bass rise a sharpe 3, the part which vses the 12 must divide, and then vse the 13, holding thesam she[4] must next vse the 10. The part which vses the 8 must hold and then descend with the false fift vnto the 3.

This holding is vppon the 11.

[fol. 23^v]

if the Bass rise a 4, and then fall a 2; or if the Bass rise a 4 and then rises another 2, or fall a sharpe 3, or a 5 the part which vses the 10 must hold, and then vse the 6, as it appeareth in the two first scores: butt in the three last the 10 holds and then vses the 6 falling downe to a 3 making a close.

This holding is vppon the 7.

[fol. 24^r]

if the Bass rise a 4, and then fall a 3 the part which vses the 10, or 17 maie hold, and then vse the 13, or 6.

This holding is vppon the 7.

[fol. 24^v]

if the Bass rise a 5 and then fall a 3, 4, or 5, or rise a 2, or 4 lett the part which vses the 15, or 8 hold, and then vse a 10, or 3.

This holding is vppon the 11, and 4.

[fol. 25ʳ]

if the Bass rise a 6 the part which vses the 12 must hold, and then vse the 13[.]

This holding is vppon the 7.

[fol. 25ᵛ]

if the Bass rise a 2, and then a 3 next falls a 2 and makes a close Canto is first to vse the 15, and then the 13[.]

[fol. 26ʳ]

if the Bass fall a 2, and then rise a 4, or 5 or fall a 3, 4, or 5, the 10 or 3 must hold next vse the 10, or 3 agayne.

The holding is vppon the 4, and 11.

[fol. 26ᵛ]

if the Bass fall a sharpe 2 in semibreves and then rise a 2 lett the part which vses the 5, or 12 divide and vse a 6, or 13 holding thesam he must vse a 6, or 13 agayne.

This holding is vppon a false 7.

[fol. 27ʳ]

if the Bass fall a sharpe 2 in minims, or chrocchets, and then rise a 2 agayne the second note of the Bass demaunds a 6 for a 5.

[fol. 27ᵛ]

if the Bass fall many seconds in semibreves or minims, the part which vses the 5 must divide, and then vse the 6, holding thesam you must vse the 6 agayne, vntill you com vnto the last note of the Bass and then the part that vses the 6 must vse the 8[.]

The holding is vppon the 7.

[fol. 28ʳ]

Or if the Bass fall manie seconds you maie beginn to devide with the 6, and then vse the 5, holding thesam you must vse the 6 agayne[.]

The holding is vppon the 6[.]

[fol. 28ᵛ]

if the Bass fall manie 2 in semibreves Canto maie hold vsing 10, and Tenor will beginn with a 5, and then vse a 6.

This waie is vsd butt seldome.

This holding is vppon the 11.

[fol. 29ʳ]

if the Bass fall a 3 and then fall a 2, or rise a sharpe 2, the part which vses the 5, or 12, must hold, and then vse the 6, or 13.

This holding is vppon the 7.

[fol. 29ᵛ]

if the Bass fall a 3 in minims or chrocchets and then rise a 2 the part which vses the 12, or 5 must hold, and next vse a 12, or 5 agayne vnto the 3 note of the Bass.

This holding is vppon a 7[.]

[fol. 30ʳ]

  if the Bass fall a 4, the part which vses the 8 must hold, and then vse the 10.
  This holding is vppon the 11, and 4.

[fol. 30ᵛ]

  if the Bass fall a 5, and then fall a 2, or rise a sharpe 2 the 3, or 10 must hold
and then vse the 6, or 13.

Sometimes you maie choose especiallie if the Bass fall a 5 in minims, or
chrocchets, and then rise a 3 as it appeareth in Canto in the last example.
  This holding is vppon the 7, and 14.

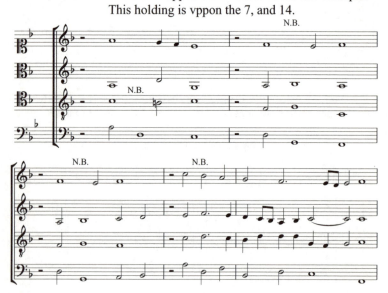

[fol. 31^r]

if the Bass fall a 5, and then rises a 3 to make a close the 10, or 3 maie hold, and next vse the 13, or 6, or elss the 3, or 10, and then come vnto the 6, or 13 agayne.

This holding is vppon the 14, and 7.

[fol. 31^v]

if the Bass fall a 4, or rise a 5 meaning for to make a staie[5] the 8, or 15 must hold, and next vse the 3, or 10.
if the Bass fall a 2, the 10, or 3 must hold[.]
if the Bass rise a 2, then the 12, or 5 must hold.
if the Bass rise a 3 the 13, or 6 must hold.

This holding consists vppon the 4, and 11.

[fol. 32^r]

How to vse a false fift.

if the Bass fall a sharpe 3, and then rise a 2, the part which vses the 3, or 10 must hold, and then com vnto the 10, or 3 agayne.
if the Bass rise a sharpe 2, and then rise another 2, the part which vses the 6, or 13 must hold, and then vse the 3, or 10.

This holding is vppon the false 5.

[fol. 32ᵛ]

How to vse a 5, and 6 together.

if the Bass rise a 2 then the 6, or 13 must hold, and then vse the 11, or 4 then holding thesam you must vse the 10, or 3, the other 6 must rise a 2, and next the 5.

if the Bass fall a 3 the 10, or 3 maie hold and then vse the 11, or 4 to com vnto the 3, or 10, holding the other 3 must rise a 2, and next vse the 5.

if the Bass rise a 4 then the part which vses the 8, or 15 must hold, and then vse the 11, or 4 to com vnto the 3, or 10 holding, the part which vses the 10 must then vse the 6, next the 5.

In the two last scores[6] you must note the Bass holding of his first note, and the next is a minim.

In the first (of the two last examples) the Bass rises a 2, and then falls a 5.

In the last the Bass rises a 4, and in these two the 6, and 5 are vsd both together in severall parts, and cleane contrarie to the other three first examples.

[fol. 33ʳ]

How to vse the 6 in steed of a 5 in a close.

The 6 in steed of the 5 is most commonlie vsd if the Bass rise to his close with seconds, or fall a 2 as it appeareth in the third score.

[fol. 33ᵛ]

How to vse a 7.

if the Bass fall a 2, 3, or 5, or rise a 2, or a 4, meaning to make a close, that part which [is] holding can vse the 7, or 14 with the Bass in the next note rising or falling, and next the 6, and then the 5.

[fol. 34ʳ]

[fol. 34ᵛ]

What chords are to be vsd

when the Bass descends seconds, and goes against the time holding his notes. if the Bass descend seconds lett Canto vse all 10, and Alto, and Tenor must goe as many 3 and 6 together to themselves as possibly they shall be able.

Hetherto the other parts have heldd vppon the Bass, now the Bass holds vppon the rest of parts.

[fol. 35ʳ]

Another waie if the Bass fall manie vneven seconds. Canto still must goe 10 with the Bass, and Tenor coms after the Bass a halfe note, first vsing a 5, and then a 6. Alto will be forced to take many vnisons with the rest of parts, by the reason of his going thorough all the parts.

[fol. 35ᵛ]

if the Bass descend seconds, and hold his first note, and the rest be minims, you maie ascend in Canto either from the 12, 10, or 8 vnto the 15 and hold vntill you can vse the 17, and then descend with the Bass in 17.

[fol. 36ʳ]

What chords are to be vsd, when the Bass ascends seconds,
and goes against the time, holding his notes.

if the Bass ascend seconds, lett Canto vse all 10, and ascend with him, and Tenor must first vse the 5, and next the 6, and must goe with the time contrarie to the Basses time.

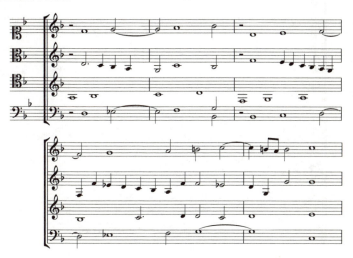

[fol. 36ᵛ]

How to maintayne a fuge.[7]

When you have chosen your fuge, you must examine all your parts, and see which of them maie beginn first, for to sooner you bring in your parts with the fuge, to more better will it shewe. After the leading part your fuges either must be brought in vppon 5, 8, 3, or vnison, and then looke on your two leading parts where you maie bring in the 3 part, and then you must lett them three goe together, untill the 4 part be brought in, being brought in you must contrive it so as that you maie convenientlie come to a close, and so leave the fuge, and goe to some other ayre, or elss some other fuge.

After the first point[8] is finishd by the Bass, or before if it [is] possible, if you will maintayne another, then what part soever be leader the rest of parts must helpe to full, and you must make a Bass of purpose for to agree with the leading fuge, and lett one part rest after another, so there be three parts still going.

[fol. 37ʳ]

Another Example.

[fols. 37ᵛ–38ʳ]

if you will twise vse the fuge in all the parts, thence you must after the Bass once hath vsd the fuge, frame him of purpose according to the parte wherin you vse the fuge, with all you must observe, that your parte maie rest rest[9] before his comming in with the fuge, which is a great grace to a part, and to the fuge.

[fols. 38ᵛ–39ʳ]

if you cannott bring in your fuge whilest the leading part is handling her[10] point, you must rest, and as soone as the point is done you must frame chords of purpose for to agree with the following part: chords for two parts must be 3, and a 6: a 5 you maie vse so you passe vnto a 3, or 6 agayne, an 8 is to be vsd in thesam manner as the 5 is. When these two parts have finishd their fuge you must force them to agree with the third part, and so you must afterwards force them to agree with the fourth part. This is now to be observed, when the fuge is nott long, nor tedious, for other it would be too single before all the parts be brought in.

[fol. 39ᵛ]

if a point be long, and tedious by the reason you vse semibreves, and minims or elss by the hardnes of the report[11] to be brought in suddenlye, you must invent another point to goe with him, first you must rest, and then com in vppon 5, 3, or 8, or vnison, with any other you must nott com in, and then you must vse 3, and 6: a 5, and 8 you maie vse so you com vnto a 3, or 6 instantlye agayne: then you must frame two parts in such sorte, that so soone as shall be possible to bring in your other two resting parts.

[fol. 40ʳ]

This fashion of maintayning of double fuges is most vsd of excellent authors, for in single fuges there can no such great art be shewed, butt onlie in the invention thereof: Besides there hath so many bene made alreadie, as that hardlie one s hall invente a single reporte to be easilie, and sweetlie brought in, butt it hath alreadie bene invented before.

Another Example.

Notes

[1] i.e., consecutive conjunct intervals.

[2] Bukofzer (p. 11 n. 37) states that in this context 'ayre' is the equivalent of 'mode'. Normally, 'ayre' would mean melody.

[3] The addition of 'seconds' above the number 2 is likely to be explanatory and is thus included in parentheses in this edition.

[4] Interesting gender switch, not however maintained except in fol. 38ᵛ.

[5] Bukofzer notes (p. 12), 'This unusual term refers to the prolongation of the bass note by means of a dot. The "stay" should not be confused with the syncope. In contrast to the latter the note making a "stay" enters on the strong beat and is held to form a half-cadence.'

⁶   i.e., bars or measures.

⁷   i.e., canon or imitative counterpoint. Coprario uses it here in the latter sense.

⁸   The melodic motif employed contrapuntally (translation of the Italian *punto*).

⁹   The word 'rest' is repeated without correction in the manuscript. This is quite obviously an error on the part of the scribe.

¹⁰   Compare fol. 23^r.

¹¹   'The entry of the consequent voice or the reiteration of the point in the various voices' (Bukofzer, p. 15).

Select Bibliography

The bibliography includes books and articles relevant to this edition but not necessarily mentioned in the Introduction or notes.

Atcherson, Walter T., 'Key and Mode in Seventeenth-Century Music Theory Books', *Journal of Music Theory*, 17 (1973), 207–33.

—— 'Symposium on Seventeenth-Century Music Theory: England', *Journal of Music Theory*, 16 (1972), 6–13.

Bathe, William, *A Brief Introduction to the True Arte of Musicke*, ed. Cecil Hill (Critical Texts, 10; Colorado Springs: Colorado College Music Press, 1979).

—— *A Briefe Introduction to the Skill of Song, c.1587*, facs. with introduction by Bernarr Rainbow (Classic Texts in Music Education, 3; Kilkenny: Boethius Press, 1982).

Benndorf, Kurt, 'Sethus Calvisius als Musiktheoretiker', *Vierteljahrsschrift für Musikwissenschaft*, 10 (1894), 411–70.

Boyd, Morrison G., *Elizabethan Music and Musical Criticism* (2nd edn, Philadelphia: University of Pennsylvania Press, 1962).

Burmeister, Joachim, *Musical Poetics*, trans. with introduction and notes by Benito V. Rivera (New Haven: Yale University Press, 1993). For a critical summary of the contents of this edition see Peter Bergquist's review in *Journal of Music Theory*, 40 (1996), 347–54.

Butler, Charles, *The Principles of Musik, in Singing and Setting (London 1636)*, facs. with introduction by Gilbert Reaney (New York: Da Capo Press, 1970).

Calvisius, Sethus, *Exercitationes musicae duae (Leipzig 1600)*, facs. edn (Hildesheim and New York: Georg Olms, 1973).

Campion, Thomas, *The Works of Thomas Campion*, ed. Walter R. Davis (New York: Doubleday, 1967; London: Faber, 1969).

—— *Campion's Works*, ed. Percival Vivian (Oxford: Clarendon Press, 1909; repr. 1966, 1967).

Charteris, Richard, 'Autographs of John Coprario', *Music & Letters*, 56 (1975), 41–6.

—— 'Jacobean Musicians at Hatfield House, 1605–1613', *Royal Musical Association Research Chronicle*, 12 (1974), 115–36.

Colles, H. C., 'Some Musical Instruction Books of the 17th Century', *Proceedings of the Musical Association*, 55 (1928–9), 31–49.

Cooper, Barry, 'Englische Musiktheorie im 17. und 18. Jahrhundert', in Wilhelm Seidel (ed.), *Entstehung nationaler Traditionen: Frankreich, England* (Geschichte der Musiktheorie, 9; Darmstadt: Wissenschaftliche Buchgesellschaft, 1986), 141–329.

Coperario, Giovanni, *Rules how to Compose*, facs. edn with introduction by Manfred Bukofzer (Los Angeles: Ernest E. Gottlieb, 1952).

Cunningham, Caroline M., 'John Coprario's Rules how to Compose and his Four-Part Fantasias: Theory and Practice Confronted', *Chelys: The Journal of the Viola da Gamba Society*, 23 (1994), 37–46.

Dahlhaus, Carl, *Studies on the Origin of Harmonic Tonality*, trans. by Robert O. Gjerdingen (Princeton: Princeton University Press, 1990).

Davis, Walter R., *Thomas Campion* (Boston: Twayne, 1987).

Descartes, René, *Compendium of Music*, trans. Walter Robert (Rome: American Institute of Musicology, 1961).

Gibbons, H., 'Observations on A New Way of Making Fowre Parts in Counterpoint by Thomas Campion' (Ph.D. diss., Harvard University, 1964).

Headlam Wells, R., *Elizabethan Mythologies* (Cambridge: Cambridge University Press, 1994).

Herissone, Rebecca, *Music Theory in Seventeenth-Century England* (Oxford: Oxford University Press, 2000).

Hulse, Lynn, 'The Musical Patronage of Robert Cecil, First Earl of Salisbury (1563–1612)', *Journal of the Royal Musical Association*, 116 (1991), 24–40.

Johnson, T. A., 'Solmization in English Treatises around the Turn of the Seventeenth Century: A Break from Modal Theory', *Theoria: Historical Aspects of Music Theory*, 5 (1990–91), 42–60.

Lester, Joel, *Between Modes and Keys: German Theory 1592–1802* (Stuyvesant, NY: Pendragon, 1989).

—— 'Major-Minor Concepts and Modal Theory in Germany, 1592–1680', *Journal of the American Musicological Society*, 30 (1977), 208–53.

—— 'Root-Position and Inverted Triads in Theory around 1600', *Journal of the American Musicological Society*, 27 (1974), 110–19.

Lewis, C. O., 'Incipient Tonal Thought in 17th-Century English Theory', *Studies in Music* (London, Ont.: University of Western Ontario), 6 (1981), 24–47.

Morehen, John, 'Thomas Snodham, and the Printing of William Byrd's *Psalmes, Songs, and Sonnets* (1611)', *Transactions of the Cambridge Bibliographical Society*, 12/2 (2001), 91–131.

Morley, Thomas, *A Plaine and Easie Introduction to Practicall Musicke*, ed. Alec R. Harman, (London: Dent, 1952; repr. 1963).

Nolte, Eckhard, *Johannes Magirus (1558–1631) und seine Musiktraktate* (Studien zur hessischen Musikgeschichte, 4; Kassel: Bärenreiter-Antiquariat, 1971).

Ornithoparchus, Andreas, *Andreas Ornithoparcus his Micrologus, or Introduction containing the Art of Singing (London, 1609)*, trans. John Dowland, facs. edn (Amsterdam and London: Da Capo Press, 1969).

—— *A Compendium of Musical Practice: Musice active micrologus / by Andreas Ornithoparchus; Andreas Ornithoparcus his Micrologus, or Introduction, containing the Art of Singing, by John Dowland. With a new introductory list of variant readings, and table of citations of theorists*, ed. Gustave Reese and Steven Ledbetter, facs. edn (New York: Dover, 1973).

Owens, Jessie Ann, 'Concepts of Pitch in English Music Theory, c.1560–1640', in Cristle Collins Judd (ed.), *Tonal Structures in Early Music* (New York: Garland, 1998), 183–246.

Pike, Lionel, *Hexachords in Late-Renaissance Music* (Aldershot: Ashgate, 1998).

Rainbow, Bernarr, 'Bathe and his Introductions to Musicke', *Musical Times*, 123 (1982), 243–7. See also: Letters to the Editor: 'Bathe', Cecil Hill, *Musical Times*, 123 (1982), 530–31.

—— *English Psalmody Prefaces: Popular Methods of Teaching, 1562–1835* (Kilkenny: Boethius Press, 1982).

Riemann, Hugo, *Geschichte der Musiktheorie im IX–XIX. Jahrhundert* (Leipzig: M. Hesse, 1898).

Ruhnke, Martin, *Joachim Burmeister: Ein Beitrag zur Musiklehre um 1600* (Kassel: Bärenreiter, 1955).

Ryding, Erik S., *In Harmony Framed: Musical Humanism, Thomas Campion and the Two Daniels* (Kirksville, Mo.: Sixteenth Century Journal Publishers, 1993).

Shirlaw, Matthew, *The Theory of Harmony* (London: Novello & Co., 1917).

Simpson, Christopher, *A Compendium of Practical Music in Five Parts (1667)*, ed. P. J. Lord (Oxford: Basil Blackwell, 1970).

Stevenson, Robert, 'Thomas Morley's "Plaine and Easie" Introduction to the Modes', *Musica Disciplina*, 6 (1952), 177–84.

Ward, John M., 'Barley's Songs without Words', *Lute Society Journal*, 12 (1970), 5–22.

Wienpahl, R. W., 'English Theorists and Evolving Tonality', *Music & Letters*, 36 (1955), 377–93.

—— 'Zarlino, the Scenario, and Tonality', *Journal of the American Musicological Society*, 12 (1959), 27–41.

Wilson, C. R., *'Words and Notes Coupled Lovingly Together': Thomas Campion, a Critical Study* (New York: Garland, 1989).

Wolf, Johannes, 'Early English Musical Theorists from 1200 to the Death of Henry Purcell', *Musical Quarterly*, 25 (1939), 420–29.

Zarlino, G., *Le istitutioni harmoniche (1558)*, facs. edn (New York: Broude Bros., 1965). Part 3 trans. Guy A. Marco and Claude V. Palisca as *The Art of Counterpoint* (New Haven and London: Yale University Press, 1968).

Zimmerman, Franklin B., 'Air, a Catchword for New Concepts in Seventeenth-Century English Music Theory', in John W. Hill (ed.), *Studies in Musicology in Honor of Otto E. Albrecht* (Kassel: Bärenreiter, 1980), 142–57.

Index